T0128226

# Motives

## Your Key to a Successful Future

G. Gilbert Cano

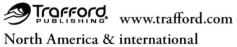

www.trafford.com
**North America & international**
toll-free: 1 888 232 4444 (USA & Canada)
fax: 812 355 4082

# Agenda

### Ideas and Concepts Presented

# Motives Action Plan

## Workbook Agenda

# Inter~Personal Communications Skills

# Preface

My sincere interest in the study of Personal Development began in the early 1980's. I was reading a copy of Success magazine when I saw an advertisement for a free copy of 'Think and Grow Rich' on cassette tape. I sent for the tape and listened, with rapt interest, to Earl Nightingale narrate an abridged version of Napoleon Hill's fantastic book. It was an epiphany to me, my first experience of listening to someone share ideas and concepts that would help me develop the self-confidence and self-motivation I needed to become a better version of myself.

I soon received a follow-up call from Success Motivation Institute to inquire about my opinion and receptivity to the information presented on the tape. My reaction was very positive. I was then invited to attend a seminar in Waco, Texas, which is only about 200 miles from my hometown. I attended the seminar, and it changed my life. I decided to get involved, on a part-time basis, and I signed a distributorship agreement and received my inventory of tapes and training programs to begin selling their products. Of course I had to listen to all the tapes, which were audio versions of the most popular business and self-improvement books at that time, so that I would be able to answer questions and make recommendations as to which tapes or programs would best meet my client's interest. I became a 'product of the product' as we used to say, and it was only the beginning. The more I listened to the tapes the more I wanted to know. I would take the profits from my sales and invest it in other programs that were available from Nightingale-Conant and other companies that produced self-improvement programs.

The self-confidence and self-esteem that is attained from reading and listening to successful people share their ideas with you is truly amazing. I feel that any money you spend on self-improvement is one of the best investments you can make. As you internalize these ideas and concepts, you find yourself making the right decisions and coming up with the right solutions to problems and they all seem to come to you naturally. Without you realizing it, your sub-conscious has been accepting the ideas and concepts you've been reading and listening to and making them available to you just when you need them. But, we will discuss this in more detail later.

In developing sales training programs I have incorporated many of the ideas and concepts I have learned. In many cases I really don't remember exactly where I first heard or read them. I do believe that the original source of almost all self-improvement ideas and concepts is Napoleon Hill's 'The Law of Success', first published in 1928.

You will find, as you listen to and read self-improvement material that many of the concepts are basically the same except that some authors will give them different names to make them seem authentic. There's nothing wrong with that. I feel that trainers and self-improvement specialist are all trying to achieve the same goal, helping people get the most out of their lives. What makes some authors truly outstanding is their ability to present ideas and concepts in a way that the majority of people can easily understand them.

I make no pretense that what I am about to share with you is original material. Except for the examples, which are based on my personal experience. 'Motive- Your Key to a Successful Future' is my attempt to share proven ideas and concepts that have been of great benefit to me, in a manner that I hope will make sense to you. I feel that the key factor in determining success, whatever success might mean to you, is to have a clear understanding of the important role that you play in determining your own future.

Although this presentation was developed as part of a Sales Training program, I sincerely hope that this presentation provides some insights into understanding the unlimited potential we all possess and will motivate you accept personal responsibility to take action to control and shape your future. We all know that we can do better than we have done in the past. What we may have lacked is that most important key element of success; a clear purpose, a powerful reason, the motivating *Motives* to do our very best.

I now share these ideas and insights with you in the optimistic hope that they will help you take advantage of this 'Do Better' opportunity, and to help you understand and develop your own powerful *Motives –* Your Key to a Successful Future'.

Enthusiastically,

*Gil Cano*

(The original slides for this presentation are in full color. The low resolution on some slides is because I chose to print in Black and White.)

I share the following ideas and insights with you in the optimistic hope that they will help you discover for yourself the advantages of having the right attitude and understand the important role you play in determining what your attitude will be. That you become aware of the most important factor in maintaining long term personal motivation, that key element of YOUR personal success story, the development your own personal and powerful…

## 'Motives'.

**Over 25 years Sales Management &
Development of Sales Training Programs**

➤ **Product Knowledge & Sales Techniques**
➤ **Technique Sales to Consultative Selling**
➤ **Inter-personal Communication Skills**
➤ **Partnership/Relationship Building**
➤ **Business/Personal Networking**
➤ **Understanding the complete Sales Process**

**Having this *Knowledge* is important to
a salesperson's *Success***

In the more than 30 years in sales, which I truly enjoyed, I have seen the change from *'technique selling'*, which was memorizing prepared sales scripts and learning somewhat manipulative sales techniques, to what is now called *'Consultative Selling'*. This important change has brought more professionalism to sales. Consultative selling requires a higher level of understanding of essential sales concepts. Concepts that will benefit not only sales reps, but anyone who has to negotiate, persuade, influence or communicate ideas to prospects, clients, family and co-workers. As I started to develop sales training programs I knew it was vitally important for anyone, especially in business, to increase their understanding of these social skills.

➤ Inter-personal Communication Skills - Learning how to communicate effectively by asking questions with a sincere interest and purpose, and actually listening to the answers to help you better understand your prospect's or co-workers real wants, needs and problems and also for clues to their decision making process.

*(These skills are so important that I have added a special section to this book, to give you a brief introduction to these concepts which I hope will develop enough interest for you to want to learn more about them.)*

➢ Partnership/Relationship Building – Finding ways to be of service to your clients beyond just making a sale. Looking for ways to work together towards the mutual benefit of both companies.

➢ Business/Personal Networking – Helping other business owners develop new relationships with some of your networking connections and with potential clients, understanding that the law of reciprocity will eventually work in your favor.

➢ Knowledge Of Your Profession –In sales, it is important for you to be as knowledgeable about your business as any other professional advisor and that you feel your service is just as important to your client's success as any other professional advice. If you don't feel your product is important, it will come across in your manner of speaking. Learning about human behavior and how it impacts the decision making process will help anyone regardless of your profession.

This information is important to your success, not only in sales, but also in your personal life.

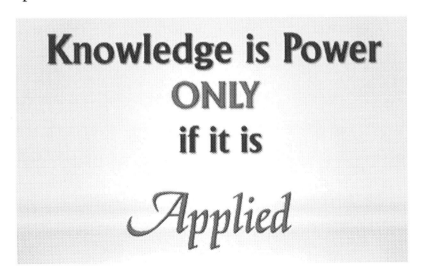

I firmly believe in the axiom that states that 'Knowledge is Power' but many people ignore the second part of the axiom which states –'… only if it is Applied'. To be able to say you attended a specific seminar or obtained a specialized certificate does not help you if you don't apply what you have learned. When you actually start applying the knowledge you have attained, only then will it be of benefit to you.

I knew I could provide the product knowledge, sales training and motivation to get the individuals excited about selling, but there is one very important aspect that needs to be addressed.

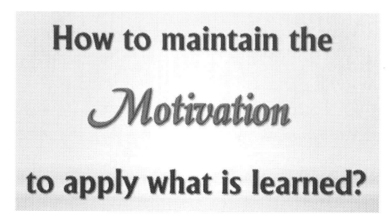

With my degree in psychology I knew exactly what I needed to do and quickly incorporated information regarding ATTITUDE into my training programs. I believe that having the right attitude is just as important, if not more important, than having the knowledge. I know some very educated individuals who have never accomplished much because they never adopted the right attitude to apply what they had learned.

This presentation is designed to help you understand the impact your attitude has on your business and personal success and the influence you have is deciding what YOUR attitude will be. Hopefully it will provide the motivation you need to move in a more positive direction.

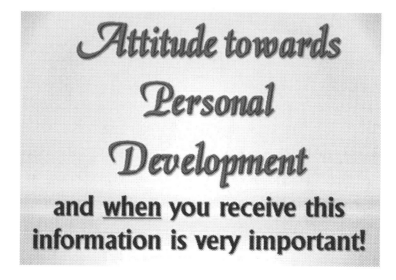

The more you understand about attitude and the influence it has on your life, the easier it will be for you to develop the unlimited potential we all possess and to become the 'Better' you. Einstein once stated that we only use about 10% of our potential, so I recognize that everyone knows in their heart that there is a better version of you; that you could do and be better if you really wanted to.

The purpose of this presentation is to help you understand how to get that 'want to' in your life. The motivation that you need to actually apply what you have learned and to work towards being the best that you can be.

I understand that timing is important. As we grow in life our priorities change. Many of the things that were important to us 5 or 10 years ago may not be as important to us now and some of the things that were not a priority then, now may have taken on more importance. The relevance of the concepts presented will depend on your individual stage of personal development and acceptance. Let me tell you a story about what happens when the timing is not right and someone is not ready to accept a new concept.

In the early-17th century, Galileo Galilei (1564 – 1642), a notable and respected scientist, learned of a telescope that was built by Dutch eyeglass makers. Taking this knowledge, he then improved on it and developed one of his own. He was soon able to determine that the Copernican theory was correct. The earth does rotate around the sun and now he could prove it. He wrote a thesis explaining his discovery, which was made public. The Church Inquisition consultants found the Copernican theory to be heretical and ordered Galileo not to "hold, teach or defend in any manner" this theory regarding the motion of the earth. The thinking was, 'How could man, who was made in the image and likeness of God, not live in the center of the universe'. When Galileo refused to deny what he knew to be true, he was found guilty of heresy and was imprisoned until he became ill. He was then confined to house arrest for the rest of his life. It was at this point that Galileo made the following statement;

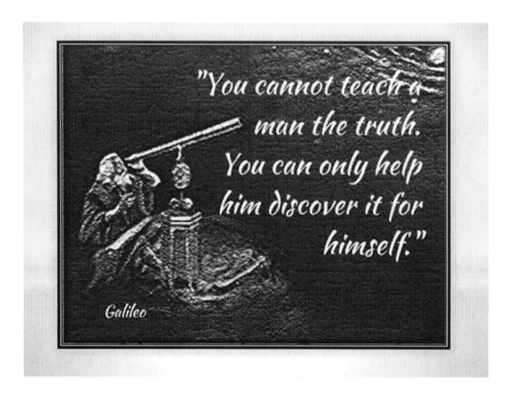

"You cannot teach a man the truth. You can only help him discover it for himself."

Galileo

I cannot imagine the pain and suffering Galileo must have endured, but I do know the feeling of wanting to share a great idea with everyone. I once had the exciting and profound opportunity to have a one on one lunch with the then President of Success Motivation Institute. During the conversation he asked if I had any questions he could answer to help me in my career with SMI. I told him that I was having trouble getting my friends to listen to the tapes. They almost seemed to avoid me, probably thinking, "Here comes Gil, wanting to talk about those tapes of his". I then asked him, "How can I get them to understand the benefits of listening to these great ideas and concepts?" He looked at me with big smile and said, "Gil, you have to learn to save the plasma for the living". I must have had a questioning look on my face because he then added; "When a person is brought into an emergency room, if there is the faintest sign of life, the first thing they do is to start pumping plasma and electrolytes into them. But, if they are 'DOA' they do not waste the plasma. If you find someone that has the slightest desire to learn and become better, then by all means give him all the help (plasma) he needs. But, if they are not interested, don't waste the plasma." I have never forgotten that and it has helped me focus on the individuals that really wanted help. Galileo's statement serves as a reminder to me that I can only share these ideas and concepts with you and hope that maybe you'll be ready to make the discovery of their benefits for yourself.

## You are an *Original.* Become your Better self.

It is a fact there is no one in the world exactly like you. There is no one that has your exact knowledge, education, training and life experiences. Therefore, you should never compare yourself or base your expectations on what anyone else has or has not been able to accomplish.

Learn all you can from mentors and successful people in your field but realize that you have the potential to take it to another level. You have everything you need to become far better than you already are. It is my goal to help you make this discovery for yourself.

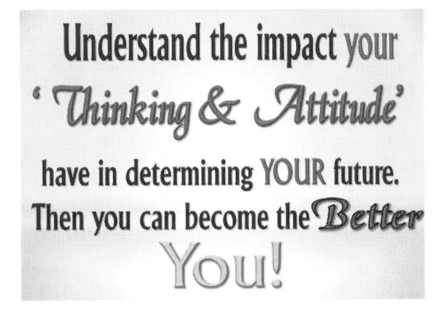

Understand the impact your '*Thinking & Attitude*' have in determining YOUR future. Then you can become the *Better* You!

> ## *Axioms for Personal Development*
> **1st** - Whether you think you can or cannot do something, you are absolutely right.
> **2nd** - Unless you try something beyond what you have already done or are doing now you will never grow and become Better.

The 1st axiom is attributed to Henry Ford. It is an essential part of the Law of Expectation which we will discuss later. A good example of this concept, at this time in our history, is evidenced almost daily; when legislators enter an important negotiation with the attitude that… "We are so far apart I don't think we will be able to reach an agreement". And guess what, they don't. One wonders what could have been accomplished if the attitude had been… "We have some differences of opinion, but I am sure we can find a way to reach a consensus." As we will learn later, our expectations do have an impact on the outcome of any course of action we entertain.

The 2nd axiom is also very important. So many people go through life repeating the same actions but expecting different results. Einstein called it 'the definition of insanity'. Don't go through life following the same routine and with the hope that things will get better. It's not going to happen by itself. Unless you decide to make a change in your routine, your life will remain the same or you will continue to fall further behind. Progress and growth are impossible without change.

There is an old saying; "When you're green you grow, when you're ripe you rot". I recommend that you don't stop growing. Don't stop looking for new ideas and concepts to improve your lifestyle, because once you think you know it all, there is no growth or progress from that point forward.

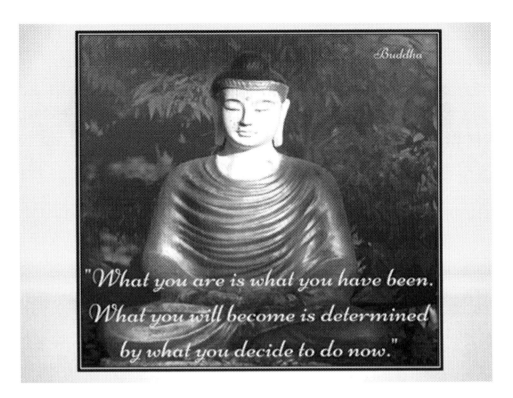

I agree. Your future is determined by choices you make starting now.

"Destiny - it's not a matter of chance, it's a matter of choice. It is not something to be waited for; it is a thing to be achieved." *W. J. Bryant*

"You're the one who has to decide, whether you'll do it or toss it aside. You are the one who must make up your mind, whether you'll lead or linger behind. Whether you'll strive for the goals that are presently far, or just be content to stay where you are. Take it or leave it there are many great things to do. Make up your mind it's all up to you." *Anonymous*

Three frogs are on a branch. Two of them decide it's to get something to eat. How many frogs are left on the branch? There's still three. To decide to do something will make no change in your life until you take action on the decision.

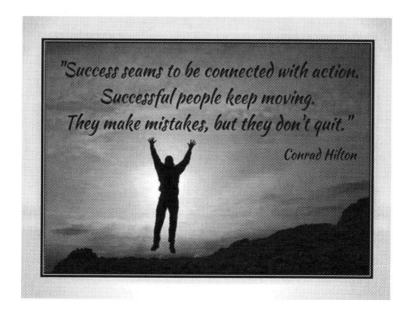

You must take action if you want to make a change and more importantly, you must persist.

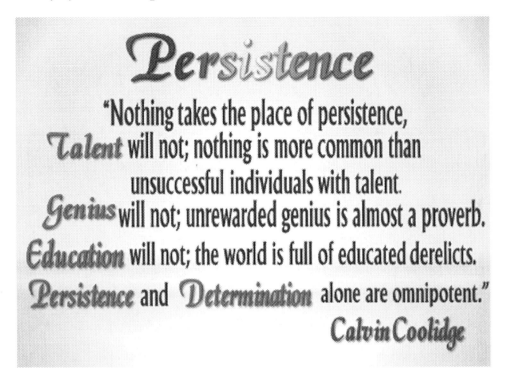

If you truly want to be BETTER, you must change the way you THINK.

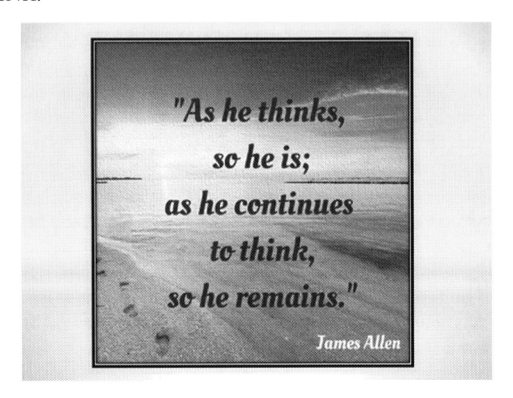

Let's take a look at some of the reasons you THINK the way you do now.

Samson was conditioned as a baby elephant not to run away by being restrained with heavy chains. Struggle as he might, he could not move beyond the length of the chain. Plus, it also hurt when he tugged at the end of the chain. So he stopped trying. Once he believed he could not move beyond the length of the chain, then, the slightest tug even from a small rope would cause him to stop.

Let me ask you this, how many times have other people's negative statements or opinions become like 'mental chains' holding you back from developing your true potential? People that we love and respected like our parents, teachers or friends that we admired, who have told us: "I didn't get past the 10<sup>th</sup> grade and I've done very well for myself" or "If that was a good idea someone else would have thought of it already" or "I know someone who tried that and failed miserably or they lost a lot of money". Though it may not have been done with malicious intent, with each negative suggestion, we start developing that negative 'chain of thought' which just keeps getting stronger, breaking our spirit so that even the slightest setback acts as 'the rope' that keeps us from moving forward. We learn to quickly rationalize our behavior, stay in our comfort zone, avoid stress and say to ourselves, "I knew that wasn't a good idea or that it wasn't going to work".

We all know that Samson could break free of that small rope that holds him if he could only recognize and believe in his true power. The same holds true for each and every one of us. We can move forward towards achieving more of our full potential when we recognize and believe in the power and control that we all truly possess in determining our own future. Someone else's opinion does not have to become your reality. You determine who you will become.

We are all created with the Equal opportunity to become UNEQUAL

I call this great opportunity a 'Special Gift' that includes the freedom of Choice.

'Special Gift'
The Unlimited Potential of the Human Mind

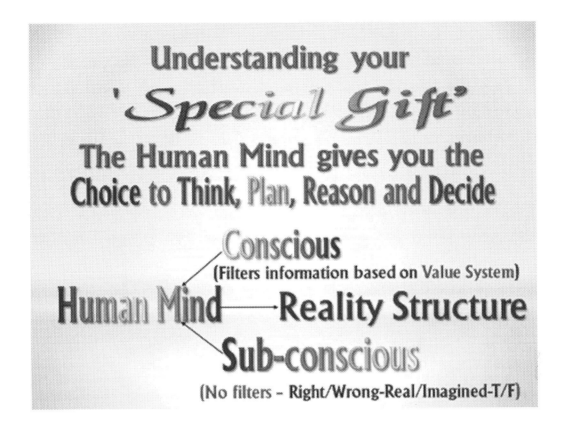

We have all been bestowed with a very 'Special Gift', the unlimited potential of the human mind. The ability to think, to plan, to reason, even the freedom of choice to decide for ourselves how much time, money and effort we want to spend in the development of this 'Special Gift'.

To take full advantage of this 'Special Gift' we must understand how it works. The human mind is extremely complex and there are many functions we still don't understand. What we do know is that it is divided into two parts the *'conscious'* and the *'sub-conscious'*. Almost everyone has heard of the psychologist Sigmund Freud. Many who study psychology do not agree with all of his conclusions. But, what has made him famous is that he was the first person to actually prove that we have a sub-conscious. Thus he is immortalized with the term 'Freudian Slip', which is when you accidently vocalize what you were thinking sub-consciously.

The *'conscious mind'* will filter information based on our value system. Our value system is what we were taught during our formative years. Our sense of what is right or wrong. This is how we were programed. Different people and different cultures have different value systems because they have been programmed differently. Unfortunately, during the first few years of our lives, we have little control over the input our mind receives.

The *'sub-conscious mind'* has no filters. It accepts all information received through all our senses without regard to right or wrong, true or false, real or imagined. It's purpose is to inform and protect the human mind and has a powerful influence on it. Your whole belief system can be changed by re-programming your sub-conscious mind.

Therefore, based on the input the sub-conscious receives, it can work for or against us. We all have heard of young individuals who have had their beliefs changed by subversive organizations. This generally stems from the need to be recognized and feel important, regardless of the organizations' purpose.

If we decide to control the information our subconcious receives with positive input, we can make it work on our behalf. This is the foundation of all 'goal setting' systems and why they do work.

The information received from our 'conscious' and 'sub-conscious' systems forms our belief system and in turn our 'Reality Structure'. We tend to make decisions and behave in a manner that is consistent with our 'Reality Structure'.

Remember that we were also given 'Freedom of Choice'. It is unfortunate that many people choose not to take full advantage of and develop their unique and powerful 'Special Gift'.

Acts can be no wiser than our thoughts. Our thinking can be no wiser than our understanding.

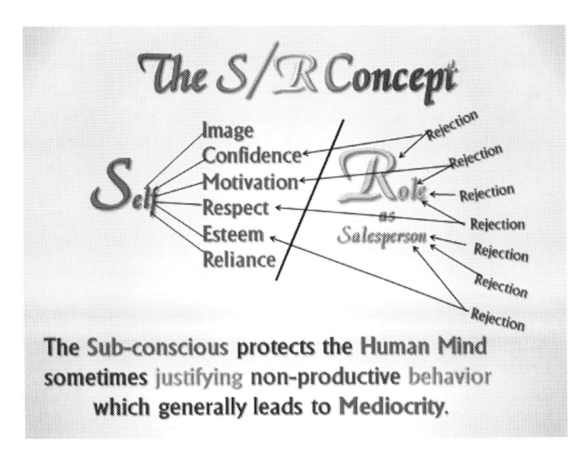

This is a slide that is designed to illustrate the negative impact the sub-conscious can have on a new salesperson's career and answers an important concern for many sales managers is... "Why is it that a new and talented sales rep, can start off so excited and end up preforming poorly after just a few months?" I'm going to spend some time on this subject because it not only affects people in sales but it is a concept that has caused many individuals to be under achievers.

The S/R concept acknowledges the SELF and shows how people who have decided to become involved in sales must understand that they are taking on an additional ROLE into their lives, like a double agent, so to speak. This new ROLE is one in which they have had no control in shaping its negative perception. Someone in sales must accept responsibility for and understand how to control the negative image that has evolved in the role of salesperson.

The SELF is the more important of the two and in which we have spent a lifetime developing. It is composed of our self-image, self-confidence, self-motivation, self-respect, self-esteem and self-reliance. It is what makes us who we are. Anything that affects the SELF, changes who we are and how we act.

The ROLE that is assumed of a salesperson carries a lot of excess baggage with it. An image that has been developed over the years and which, unfortunately, is not a very positive one. For the most part, this image is well deserved because of former sales merchants who made a living swindling people. Between the two roles, there is a barrier (/), which keeps them separated. This barrier is extremely important!

When someone starts in the ROLE of a salesperson, he or she will begin to receive some rejection, such as; "don't need it", "not interested", "don't bother me", "already have a vendor", "no thank you", etc… I know that with proper training a lot of this rejection can be reduced; but unfortunately, many sales reps never receive the proper training. The important thing to remember is that this rejection is not aimed at you personally. They don't even know who you are. It is aimed at the ROLE you are playing of a salesperson.

When this rejection starts to cross the 'barrier' it begins to affect your SELF. Your self-confidence stars to slip and your self-esteem takes a hit. This is when the sub-conscious steps in to protect your SELF by giving you justification to avoid the rejection. You begin to make excuses like; "Its Friday no one is in their office" or "It's Monday they're busy planning the new week" or "Everyone says our prices are too high" or "I can already tell he won't be interested, so why waste my time". All of these non-productive excuses are coming from your sub-conscious which is just trying to protect your SELF.

So how do you stop this downward spiral which only ends with you not being as successful as you could be or not developing to your full potential? You strengthen the barrier between the SELF and the ROLE (S/R) by learning more about human behavior and why people react the way they do. By reading books on self-improvement and learning more about how to improve your inter-personal communication skills for business and personal relationships. This way when you receive rejection, and you will, it will be of no surprise to you and you will already know how you are going to respond to it in a positive way.

I hope this little discourse makes sense to you. Many potentially good sales reps and entrepreneurs have become under achievers and are doomed to mediocrity because they did not understand this concept.

*Mediocrity* is achieved by 'Pleasing Methods'. This means doing only the things that feel comfortable to us, staying within our 'comfort zone'. Doing only what makes us feel good and what helps us avoid stress.

*Success* is achieved by 'Pleasing Results'. This requires us to do whatever it takes to get the results we want. Sometimes the actions that need to be taken require us to step outside of our 'comfort zone'. It may also require us to take actions that might be stressful. Doing whatever it takes is not always the easiest action to take. But, it is the most rewarding.

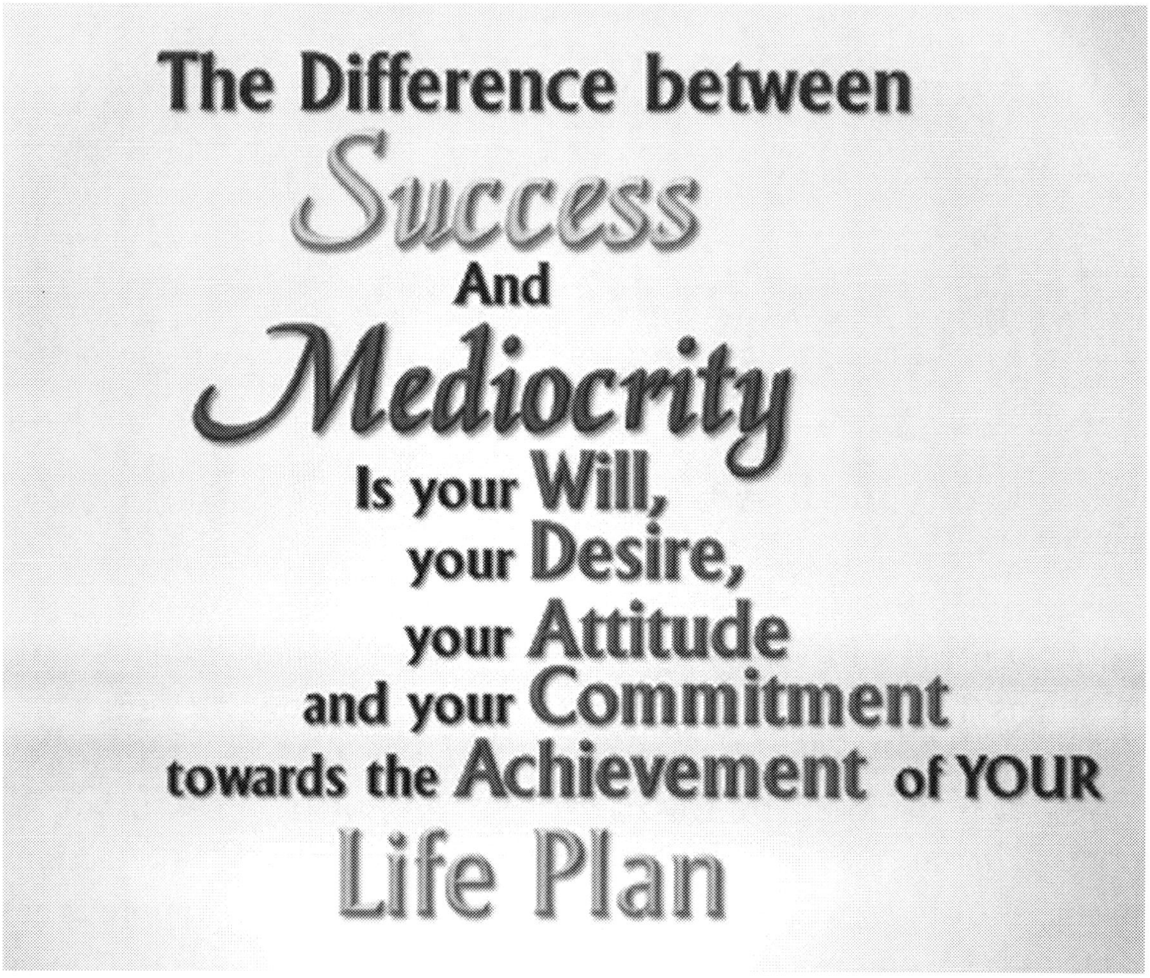

The Difference between

*Success*

And

*Mediocrity*

Is your **Will,**
your **Desire,**
your **Attitude**
and your **Commitment**
towards the **Achievement** of **YOUR**

Life Plan

**The Essence of a Life Plan**

➢ Starts with a decision to take Action
➢ Allows Self-Appraisal & control of Input
➢ Provides direction for your Goals
➢ Allows to incorporate Affirmations
➢ Clarify objectives using Visualizations
➢ Tap into Universal Energy/Vibrations

*You make your Sub-conscious Work for You!*

I think a Life Plan is essential because it is the most effective way to get your *'sub-conscious'* to work for you in a positive way. It all starts with your decision to commit to take positive action towards the achievement of your life goals. A Life Plan will allow you to take control of the input your sub-conscious will receive. There are several important steps to making effective life plan. Using a Life Coach can be very helpful.

*(These important steps are outlined and explained in more detail in the* **'Action Plan'** *section of this book.)*

After going through a series of exercises to help you determine what you really want to achieve or obtain, you will be able to write your most important *Goal Statements.*

The next step is to clearly write down the *Benefits Received from Achievement* and the negative *Consequences of Non-Achievement* of your goal. The benefit of a gain and/or the fear of a loss are two very important motivating factors.

Then give some thought to *Possible Obstacles* that might delay the achievement of your goal and *Possible Solutions for Obstacles* to help eliminate unexpected setbacks.

Your plan should incorporate written *Affirmations*, which are your goals stated as if they are already achieved, and should be read out loud daily to help keep you and your sub-conscious on target.

Dividing your goals into *Action Steps for Achieving this Goal*, allows you to monitor your progress. As you see progress being made, you start believing in yourself and in your ability to achieve your goals. This will increase your self-confidence to overcome minor setbacks and give you determination to persist.

Incorporate the power of *Visualization*, which are photos or visual reminders of your goal, so that you can maintain a clear picture in your mind of what you want to accomplish and why you are going through this process.

Tapping into the *Universal Energy/Vibrations* is hard to explain. I do know they exist. I'm going to share with you how I learned this. One day during a course I was taking in Para-psychology our professor asked, if anyone was interested in attending a performance by a psychic named Uri Geller to stay after class so we could purchase tickets to all sit together. Geller had supposedly fallen from a tree when he was a child and landed on his head. It caused a change in his brain which gave him paranormal powers. During his performance he was known to ask his audience to bring any watch that quit working to the stage and he would repair it by just holding it and sending cosmic energy to it. The professor had bought a very ornate pocket watch in Mexico and had gotten it very cheap because it did not work. He thought he would bring it to Houston and have it repaired. What he found was that the company that built the watch went out of business during WWII and parts were not available, so it never had worked. We were going to take the watch to the performance just to see if Geller could make it work. When the time came, we took the watch to the stage and along with several other watches and put it on a chair. Geller stood over the chair, made a theatrical gesture and said they were repaired. After the performance one of us went to get the watch; brought it back to the professor who opened the pocket watch and we all saw that it was working. Don't ask me to explain how it happened but I do know that we deliberately wanted to see if he could really draw on cosmic energy and we found out he could. This was proof to me why the Law of Attraction does work.

At the very bottom of the action plan worksheet there is a question.

*Is it worth my time, money and effort to reach this goal?*

If this question cannot be answered with a resounding YES, then this goal is not that important to you and your chances of achieving it are seriously diminished. You must start with a goal that is important to you so that you will have the incentive to follow through the whole process. Once you achieve that first important goal and you understand that the process does work, subsequent goals are a cinch.

Let me share some thoughts as to how others have thought about planning one's life:

*Funny thing about life: If you refuse to accept anything but the best, you very often get it.* Somerset Maugham

*Life is like a bank account. You only get back what you put in. Experience is the interest.*

*Life can be spent waiting for the storm to pass or we can learn to dance in the rain.*

*Life is a play! It's not its length, but its performance that counts.* Seneca

*There are three essentials in life; something to do, someone to love, and something to hope for.*

*It's not so much where we are that's important, but in what direction we are moving.*

*If one does not know to which port one is sailing, no wind is favorable.* Seneca

*There is no such thing in anyone's life as an unimportant day.* Alex Woollcott

*You don't get to choose how you are going to die or when. You can only decide how you're going to live.* Joan Baez

*It is not the years in your life but the life in your years that count.* Adlai Stevenson

*Don't let yesterday take up too much of today.* *Will Rodgers*

*If you are working on something that you really care about, you don't have to be pushed. The vision pulls you.* – *Steve Jobs*

I have often heard, "Okay, I have tried this before and did not get the expected results" Maybe the timing in your life was not right; or maybe you did not approach it with the right attitude and did not make the commitment to persist.

Often I've been asked, "Tell me specifically, how will I know when I am really ready to make the commitment to take action and get started on developing my Life Plan?"

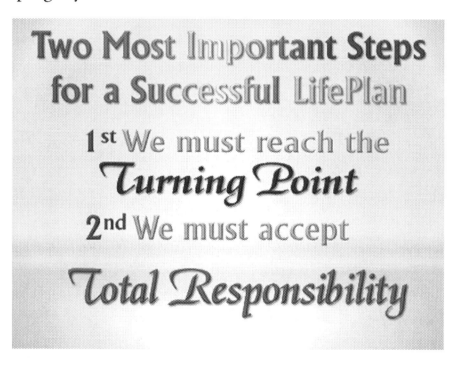

To become truly **Unequal**, the first step is to reach the 'Turning Point' in your life. That moment when you can honestly say to yourself, "I know that I can do better than I have been doing and I want to discover what I can truly accomplish if I gave it a sincere effort. I know that I have undeveloped potential and I will make a commitment to focus on learning how to maximize my efforts in its development".

The next step is accepting 'Total Responsibility' for what happens to us. Accepting 'Total Responsibility' is the most important sign of maturity. Unfortunately, some people go through life never accepting 'Total Responsibility' for their actions. As it is often said, 'Puberty only lasts through adolescence but immaturity can last a lifetime'. The main sign of immaturity is blaming other people or circumstances for what happens to us. Do you know anyone with this attitude? Putting the blame elsewhere is very convenient. As long as we continue to blame other people, we never have to make changes in our own actions. The thinking is 'Why should I change, it's not my fault'.

Let me share a personal story that demonstrates what taking responsibility is all about. When my son joined the USAF he went to basic training at Lackland AFB in San Antonio. After his third week, he was allowed to have visitors, so my wife and I went to have lunch with him. When we asked how things were going, he said, "To tell you the truth, I got my butt chewed out this morning. We had an inspection before we were allowed to leave and I had a small thread sticking out of my lapel. My TI then proceeded to get in my face and at the top of his lungs screamed that the cables that were hanging from my uniform showed that I had no respect for my uniform or the United States Air Force, and then proceeded to put on KP".

My son then said something that let me know he was going to do just fine. He said, "It was my fault. I should have known better. I could have been more careful. It will never happen again". He was taking control of the situation and putting that responsibility on himself.

Without taking 'Total Responsibility' we give other people and circumstances control of our lives. As I mentioned earlier, this is why having a 'Life Plan' is so essential. If you don't have a plan to take control of your life, someone else will do it for you and they might not have your best interests at heart.

Without a Plan, you're like a ship without a rudder. You may be smart, beautiful and powerful but you'll never get out of the port. Accepting 'Total Responsibility' and accountability for developing your life's plan provides the rudder. A 'Life Plan' is the map that helps you navigate towards your desired destination. The truth of the matter is that most people will spend more time planning a vacation than planning for their future. For instance, they will get on the internet and see the places of interest that are close by their destination that they don't want to miss. Along with their suitcases, they pack their days full of places to go and things to see.

Question - Don't you think that making the most of the 'days of your life' deserves a little attention? Shouldn't you take a little time to think about some of the things you would like to do, to have, to become; knowing you can develop a plan to turn you wants into reality?

Accept TOTAL RESPONSIBILITY for your life and know that YOU control your future, no one else. A 'Life Plan' gives you purpose and a reason to persist and 'Persistence, as we learned, is very important'.

I am often asked, "If all it takes to be successful is to write down your goals; then why is it that so few individuals are truly successful?" First of all, it is not just writing down your goals, it is also the commitment and the persistence in taking action towards achieving them.

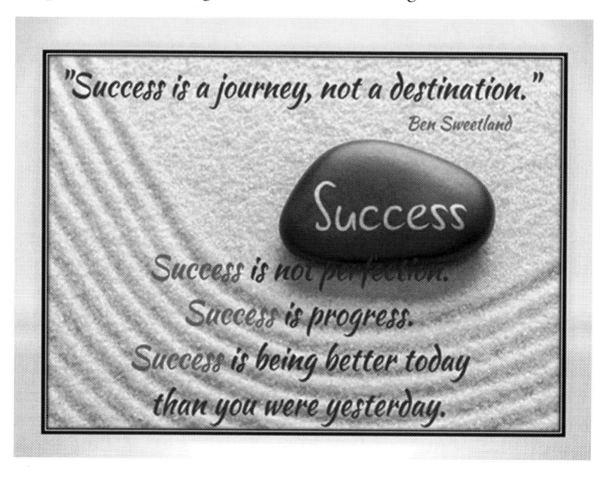

**Here are some thoughts on Success;**

*All success comes from daring to begin.*

*You're on the road to success when you realize that failure is merely a detour.*

*If at first you don't succeed, you're running about average.*

*Success is just a matter of failures, overcoming them.*

*There is a six word formula for success: Think things through, and then follow through* -Rickenbacker

*The people who try to do something and fail are infinitely better than those who try to do nothing and succeed.*

*To succeed, don't learn the tricks of the trade; learn the trade.*

**Here are a few thoughts on life:**

*There are three ingredients in the good life: learning, earning and yearning. - C. Morley*

*You are not a mere passenger on the train of life; you are the engineer.*

*Life is a horse, and either you ride it, or it rides you. – Gregory McDonald*

*Most of the great things in life are one-syllable things; peace, love, joy, trust, home, hope.*

*The trick is growing up without growing old. - Casey Stengel*

*Three words sum up what you can count on in life. It goes on.*

*Life is what happens to you while you are making other plans.*

*Don't let life get away. Just when you learn to make the most of it, most of it is gone.*

*The essential ingredient of life is timing. There is no time like the present.*

*The business of life is to go forward. Nothing is as good or as bad as it appears.*

*Life is like a menu. It's not very exciting if you eat the same thing every day.*

*All men should strive to learn before they die, what they are running from, and to, and why. – James Thurber*

**Your Success is determined by the choices You make.**

*Law of Accident*

or

*Law of Cause and Effect*

I've often heard, "Failure to plan is a plan for failure." I honestly feel that preparing a good Life Plan can help you achieve many goals that you might want to accomplish and that, maybe, you were just not convinced that you had the power to do so. Most people gauge success by how much money you make. Don't fall into that mindset. Do yourself a favor, and go through the preliminary exercises in the *Action Plan* that focus on helping you get a clear picture of where you are now. This self-appraisal lets you evaluate the important areas in your life. Such as: Physical, Intellectual, Social, Financial, Spiritual and Family Relationships. If after going through the exercise you are completely satisfied with your life as it is, then, I sincerely congratulate you.

**Law of Accident**

**95%** choose to live by this Law
- Don't plan to fail, just fail to plan
- Let circumstances dictate future
- Hope they'll get lucky - catch a break
- Often demonstrate **Negative Behavior**

But, if you choose to live by the 'Law of Accident' and let circumstances dictate your future, believing that maybe you'll get lucky and win the lottery or that you'll be at the right place at the right time and get that big break you need, then your success will truly be by accident. If you choose not to be proactive only because you fear that you might fail in the attempt to improve your lifestyle, then, I do believe that you are only failing yourself.

You must learn to view an unexpected setback as sign to try again some other way. A guided missile, aimed at a target, has to make adjustments along the way. It cannot make adjustments until it is launched. The missile can only make adjustments while it is moving. Just don't ever give up on developing your true potential. You can only fail if you give up on yourself and quit trying. As long as you pick yourself up and try again some other way, as long as you keep moving forward, you will never be a failure. We have seen that people choose to live in mediocrity just because they don't want to leave their 'comfort zone'.

One of my favorite quotes on knowing what you want, the importance of believing in yourself and accepting failure as a part of being successful is:

*"I've missed more than 9000 shots in my career. I've lost more than 300 games. 26 times I was trusted to take the game winning shot and missed. I've failed over and over and over again in my life. And that is why I succeed."- Michael Jordan*

Let me show you how to leave the world of *Mediocrity* behind and move forward towards a more successful future.

Avoid Negative Behavior. Do not be pessimistic, always visualizing the worst that could happen. If you do not attempt to do something because everything is not perfect, and you fear you might fail, then you are already defeated.

Replace with Positive Behavior. Be optimistic and imaginative. Look for the action steps of your Life Plan that can be completed now. Do not be content to stay in your comfort zone. If you continue doing what you have been doing, nothing will change. Use your imagination to move forward and try something different. If you want more out of life, YOU must be willing to do more than you have been doing.

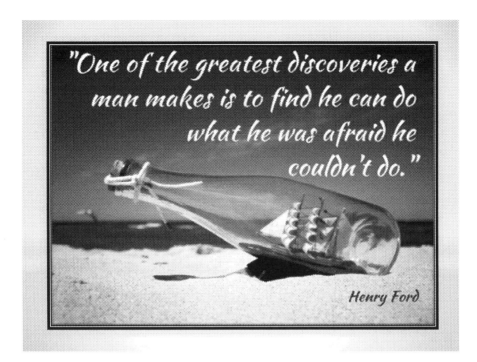

Your Desire for Success must always be greater than your Fear of Failure.

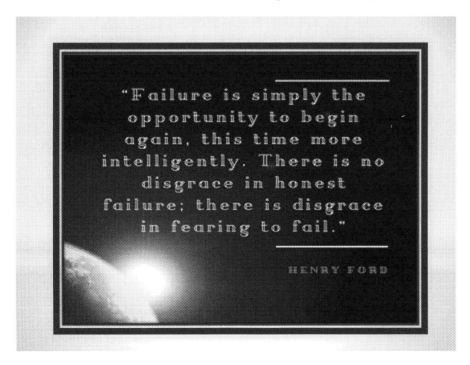

Be optimistic and look for the action steps of your Life Plan that can be completed now. Use your imagination to move forward and try something different than what you have been doing.

## Law of Cause and Effect
## Only 5% choose to live by this Law.
- Every effect has a cause
- Identify the cause to produce the desired effect
- Thoughts are causes – results are effects
- What we *Think* becomes results/effects

### Develop a Plan of Action using the cause to produce the desired effect!

Every time I see this statistic, I say to myself, "This can't be true. There must be more than 5% who understand this Law." But try as I might, I cannot find evidence to refute it. So let's see if I can find a way to explain it so it can make sense and you can take full advantage of it.

Once you have determined your goal, which is the condition or effect you want to achieve, you then develop a *'Plan of Action'* using the causes that you have identified as *'Action Steps'*, to produce the desired effect or goal.

What makes this process so successful, and what most people tend to forget, is that by putting our *'Plan of Action'* in writing we have an opportunity to read and think about our *'Action Steps'* and that thoughts are causes and what we think becomes conditions or effects. To put it another way;

# 'We Become What We Think About'

Are you skeptical about the statement that 'We Become What We Think About'? Allow me to explain.

The way we *ACT* is a manifestation of our belief system and our reality structure. It is also a reflection of our self-image, self-confidence and self-esteem.

Our *PERSONALITY* is how people describe the way we act.

The personality is a reflection of our *ATTITUDE*. A person with a positive attitude is described as having an exciting, fun-loving, enjoyable and optimistic outlook. A person with a 'great to be around' personality.

A person with a negative attitude is described as having a boring, pessimistic and depressing personality. Someone you want to avoid.

Our attitude is influenced by our *FEELINGS* regarding certain topics, towards certain people, places or things, our Reality Structure.

Our feelings are determined by the *THOUGHTS* we entertain.

Therefore, what we think about will eventually determine how we will *ACT*.

It is a fact, 'We Become What We Think About'. If we expand our level of thinking we can expand our level of being. Or put another way, elevate your thinking and you elevate yourself.

One explanation as to why this is true is based on the concept that our thoughts have a specific wavelength that is picked up by our subconscious. The strength of these thought waves is based on our degree of belief, the stronger our belief the more powerful the results based on them. We know that there are numerous soundwaves all around us but you need a radio or TV receiver to be able to hear or see them. Our subconscious is our built-in thought wave receptor. Make sure your thoughts are positive and focused on what we want to have or become.

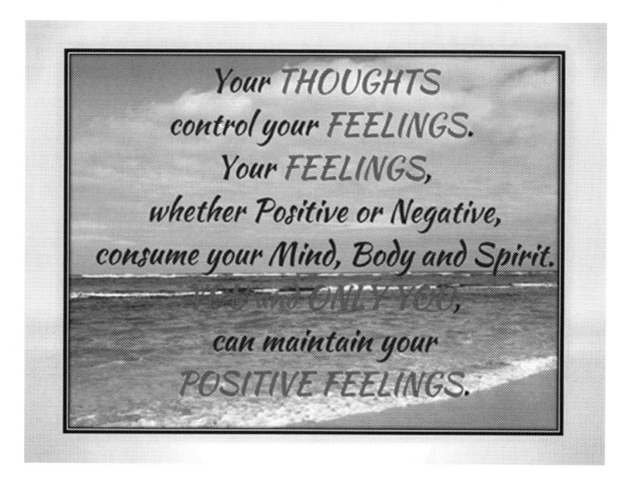

Here are some ideas on thought by some famous people.

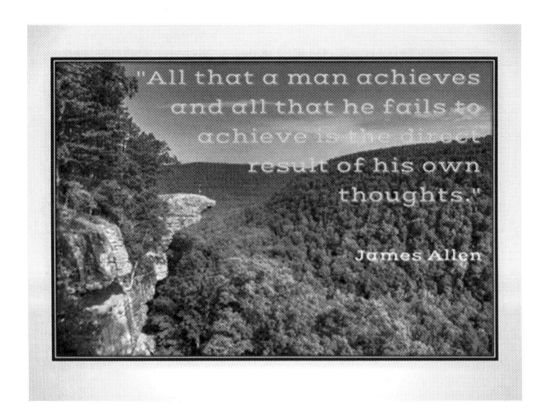

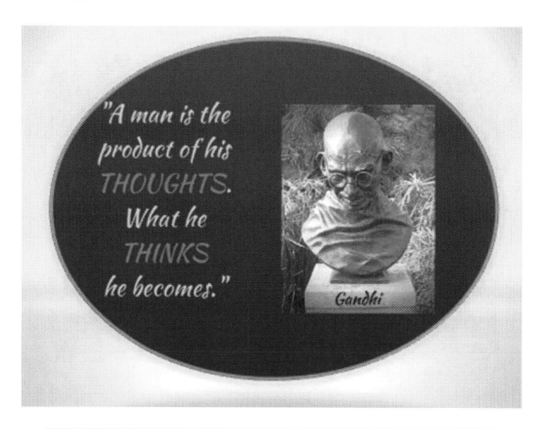

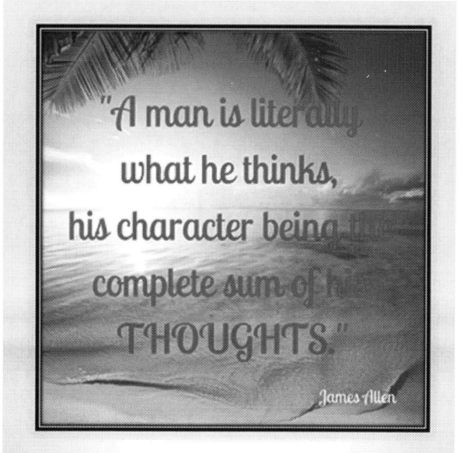

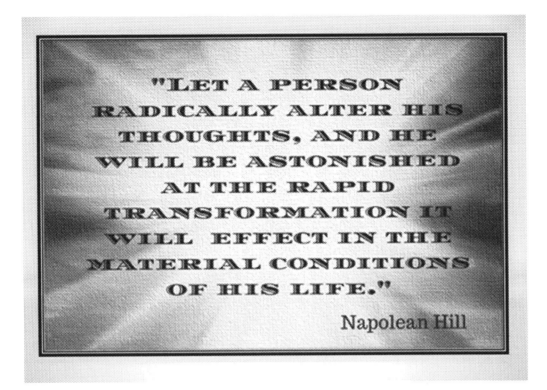

"LET A PERSON RADICALLY ALTER HIS THOUGHTS, AND HE WILL BE ASTONISHED AT THE RAPID TRANSFORMATION IT WILL EFFECT IN THE MATERIAL CONDITIONS OF HIS LIFE."

Napolean Hill

You want to be mindful of your thoughts and choose them carefully because they are creating your future. Avoid any negative thinking. When you start thinking positively, you will find how much more you will enjoy life.

**The 3 most important Laws of the Mind**

**Law of Belief**

**Law of Expectation**

**Law of Attraction**

The 'Laws of the Mind' have such an impact on our lives; there are several. I want you to be aware of three of the most important. They are: Law of Belief, Law of Expectation and the Law of Attraction.

These 'Laws' much like the Laws of Nature work 100% of the time and just because you don't know them or believe in them does not mean they will not affect you. If you jump off a cliff you will go down, even if you don't know about the Law of Gravity.

**Law of Belief**

What we *Believe* becomes our *Reality Structure*.

Our actions are influenced by the Degree of our Belief.

4 Degrees of Belief    1st ~ Opinion (soft)

2nd ~ Bias (firm)

3rd ~ Judgment (strong)

4th ~ Conviction (solid)

Must change *Belief Structure* to change *Reality Structure*.

We have learned that our 'Special Gift', is greatly influenced by input received from the conscious and sub-conscious minds, and that this input forms our belief system. We also learned that what we believe becomes an essential part of our 'Reality Structure'. Our actions are then influenced by the degree of our belief.

There are 4 degrees or levels of belief:

> 1st – Opinion – this degree of belief is the weakest. It can be swayed by receiving more information on the subject.
>
> 2nd – Attitude – this level is harder to change; it has been influenced by our personal life experiences, but, our attitude can be changed if we choose to do so.
>
> 3rd – Judgment – these are strong beliefs involving controversial concepts such as politics, abortion, gun control, gay marriage, etc. Judgments can be changed but it would require a lot of believable evidence to do so.
>
> 4th – Conviction – This is the strongest level of belief, one that we will defend with our lives if necessary.

We know that we must change our belief system in order to change our 'Reality Structure'. If you have any doubts or reservations regarding your ability to grow and become better, these beliefs must be changed. We must believe in ourselves and believe that we have the power to change our lives. We must believe this with *Conviction*.

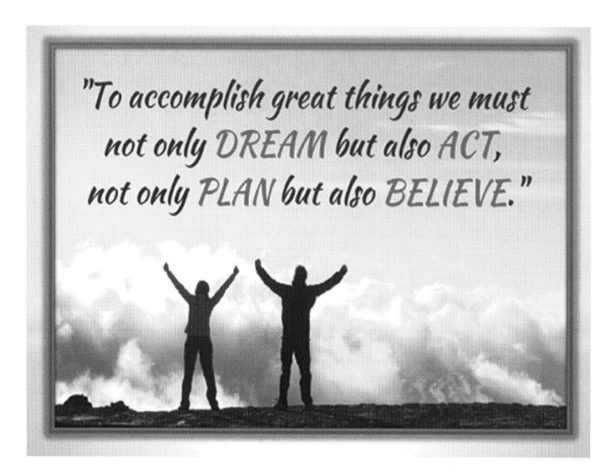

## Law of Expectation

### Expect to Fail

-You Look for excuses and justification

### Expect to Succeed

-You Look for opportunities and solutions

When you approach a new negotiation, a new project, a new position or any new undertaking with the expectation to succeed, you will have a very positive attitude and will be constantly looking for ways to make the outcome successful. There can be no doubt in your mind and in your heart that you will succeed and this will give you the power to persist and never give up. Expect the best and you will very often achieve it.

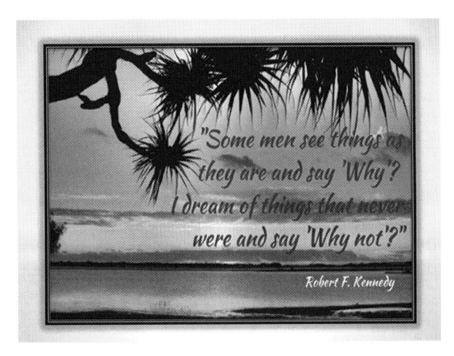

"Some men see things as they are and say 'Why'? I dream of things that never were and say 'Why not'?"

Robert F. Kennedy

*Law of Attraction*
We attract to ourselves the people and the circumstances that harmonize with our *Dominate Thoughts.*

We become *Living Magnets* of opportunity.

A few years ago, a book was released called 'The Secret'. When I first heard about it I was very impressed with the people who endorsed the book. When I read the book I realized the book was an updated perspective of the 'Law of Attraction', I understood why people were ready to endorse it. The 'Law of Attraction' really does work. There is no doubt about it.

Are you familiar with what is called the 'Cocktail Party Phenomenon'? This takes place when, in the midst of several conversations taking place in a room, someone happens to mention your name. Like radar, you can hear your name clearly spoken. You might even excuse yourself from your present conversation to go see who was talking about you. That is how the 'Law of Attraction' works. When you have written goals that you read daily and are thinking about them every day, they become part of your 'Dominate Thoughts' and you can pick them up out of the air. These thoughts will attract the people and circumstances that harmonize with them. We become 'Living Magnets' of opportunity.

When I was younger, I had owned a Datsun 240Z, then a 280Z 2+2. Then Nissan came out with a 280ZX 2+2. They were dual colored and one combination was blue and silver like the Dallas Cowboys. *(I told you I was from Texas.)* I really wanted one but could not afford it at the time. So I put it on my list and I had pictures of exactly the one I wanted. One day I was in a tavern with some friends of mine that were in the used car business when I overheard someone, at another table, say they had just picked up a wrecked 280ZX 2+2 that was rear ended. I went to that table, inquired about the condition, bought it, sent it to a friend's body shop, and within a couple of weeks I was driving my dream car. Everyone said I was so lucky. I knew it came from the 'Law of Attraction'. It is important to realize that Thoughts, Actions and Emotions all aligned in a positive direction, compound their energies with one another. You will receive more of what you THINK about, TALK about and FEEL strongly about.

You hold the to unlock the power of the Law of Attraction in your Thoughts, Emotions, Affirmations, Visualizations, and your Actions.

## You determine *Who* you are and *Where* you are in life, by the *Dominating Thoughts* that occupy your mind.

Here is the key that makes understanding this concept so important. WE control our thoughts; therefore, WE can determine who we will become. Let me give you quick example of how to use this concept to your advantage.

## Do *You* have a *Clear* and *Specific Idea* of what *You* really want to Do, to Have and to Become?

The main reason most people get so little out of life is that they don't know what they really want. There is a quote I once heard that has always intrigued me; "Most people go through life aiming at nothing and hitting it with amazing accuracy."

When asked what they want out of life, many people will use very general and non-specific terms like; I want to be happy, I want to be successful, I want to be rich, I want to travel, etc. All great wants but not very motivating because they are not clear and specific. When I hear these kinds of statements I will ask questions to get them to clarify these wants: "What will it take specifically to make you happy?" Or "What specifically needs to happen so that you will know you are successful?" Or "Specifically, how much money will it take for you to consider yourself rich?" Or "Where specifically would you like to go?" I then keep asking clarifying questions until they end up with a specific idea of what needs to be done to accomplish that want.

Identifying and crystalizing you goals is not a very difficult process but extremely important to the concept of developing a 'Life Plan'. It is how you develop an *Action Plan* to achieve your goals.

As the often quoted 'philosopher' Yogi Berra once said, "You've got to be very careful if you don't know where you're going, because you might not get there."

Having a clear vision of what you WANT is essential to your success in it's achievement.

Don't confuse *Wishes* & *Wants*

When you merely wish for something you just sit and wait and hope it comes to you. You allow the 'Law of Accident' to decide your future. I once read; "A lot of people spend half their time wishing for things they could have, if they didn't spend half their time wishing."

When you really want something, you put the 'Law of Cause and Effect' into action and determine want it is going to take to get what you want. Then with all your heart and soul you put your mind into action and go for it.

You may have done it before without realizing it. Has there ever been someone very special to you that you really wanted to meet? Didn't you spend time trying to find that person's schedule so that you could 'accidently' be there to have a friend casually introduce you? You went through all the trouble because you really wanted to make it happen. You had a motive.

Here are some thoughts on taking action and overcoming setbacks:
*People judge you by your actions, not your intentions. You may have a heart of gold, but so does a hard-boiled egg.*

*You can't plow a field by merely turning it over in your mind.*
*A positive anything is better than a negative nothing.* E. Hubbard

Let me explain why knowing what you want can be a very motivating factor in your life.

When you have determined what you really WANT, the goal you want to achieve, it is then possible to develop a PLAN, with a series of action steps, which you will follow to reach the goal. With a clear idea of what you want and a specific plan to attain it, you will develop an 'I can do that' attitude. With this attitude, you will develop the DESIRE and the commitment to overcome minor setbacks and focus on the plan. This desire will give you the CONFIDENSE to outperform even your own expectations and more importantly it will strengthen your ability to BELIEVE IN YOURSELF. You may accomplish great things even if no one else believes in you, but never, if you do not BELIEVE IN YOURSELF.

Remember: The exercises provided in the *ACTION PLAN part* of this book; will help provide an honest Self-Appraisal which will help you determine what areas in your life you deem important to improve. This will also help you determine what you really WANT out of life.

Let me give you the added super-bonus from knowing what you truly want, it is the essential key ingredient to long term, self-sustained, Personal Motivation.

**Knowing what you** *Want* **gives you a** *Motive* **to take** *Action.* *Action* **taken on a** *Motive* **is** *Motivation!*

Have you ever noticed that all the detectives in the criminal TV series always look for someone who has a motive to commit the crime? They understand that no one will take major action without a motive. For someone to take action there must be a benefit they will receive; the greater the benefit the stronger the motive to take action.

When you take the time to determine what you truly want out of life and set a goal with a plan of action for its attainment; that goal will serve as the motive for you to take action. This is why a person with a great Life Plan is always motivated.

Want > Goal > Motive > Action.

To put it another way; knowing what you want gives you a motive to take action. And, action taken on a motive is motive-action or motivation. A well written Life Plan will help give you *Motives -Your Key to a Successful Future!*

Let's look at a system one man used to turn a WANT into a reality.

## The Da Vinci Code

### The 'SMART' System

S - **Specific:** define exactly what you want

M - **Measurable:** Plan recognizable benchmarks

A - **Accountability:** Commit to be responsible

R - **Realistic:** Achievable and relevant

T - **Timeline:** Set a timeline for achievement

Leonardo DaVinci is said to have developed a system to help him define and achieve goals. He used the system religiously every time he began a new project and called it the SMART system. I feel that the acronym is easy to remember and serves an easy reference to see if your goal is well defined. It should be:

*Specific* – You should be able to define exactly what you want to achieve.

*Measurable* – You should be able to set recognizable benchmarks that will allow you to check your progress and keep you excited and on track.

*Accountability* – It should be important enough so that you can commit to take actionable steps towards its achievement.

*Realistic* – If you cannot define measurable actions steps that you know you can achieve, then it is probably not a realistic or achievable goal.

*Timeline* – you must set a realistic timeline for its achievement to help avoid procrastination and to give you feedback on your progress.

There are individuals who avoid setting a goal because they feel that if you don't achieve it on time that you have failed. This is not true. The timeline is set for your benefit, to help you validate your progress.

Sometimes there are things that we have not taken into consideration when setting the timeline. When you have identified these minor setbacks and a solution to get past them, then just reset you timeline and continue towards the achievement of your goal.

## What kind of person will I have to become to get the things I *Want?*

You have learned that you cannot continue to do the same things and expect different results. Progress and growth are not possible without change. In order to get the things you WANT, you have two choices:

Change the person that you are
Or
Change the things that you want.

You now know that you can decide the kind of person you want to become, because you control your thoughts and you know 'We Become What We Think About'.

You just need to think the thoughts that will make you the type of person who will follow through on the commitments you have made to follow your Life Plan. Remind yourself that you will fulfill your commitments because the commitments you have made are worth fulfilling.

I've heard it said, "If you want to have more YOU have to become more."

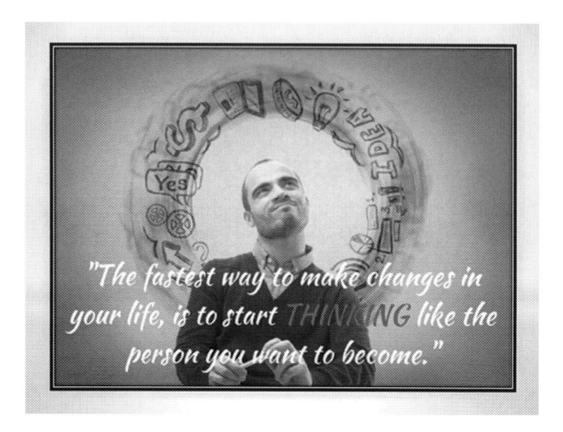

"The fastest way to make changes in your life, is to start THINKING like the person you want to become."

The main reason for lack of progress on a job is that people work on the job and not on themselves. If you aspire to a better position within the company, make sure you are ready when the opportunity presents itself.

Here is the 'key' to being ready. Start right NOW thinking and acting like the kind of person they would be looking for in the position you desire to attain. Ask yourself: How would a responsible and successful person in that position respond to this problem, address this issue or handle this situation? Then, you must start doing and acting accordingly. You may want to volunteer to help someone in that position whenever possible so that you can get OJT experience in the position.

Always remember: Nothing is permanent, circumstances will change, people will be promoted or retire or leave the company for a better position. Opportunities will become available and you can capitalize on them because you will be ready. You will be a top choice, because you already think and act like that responsible person they are looking for to fill that position.

You can expect criticism from people who are so afraid of failure they don't even want to attempt to improve their lifestyle but they will try to dissuade you from doing so. They don't want you to leave them behind; they do not want you to succeed. They truly do not have your best interest at heart.

**Provide more service than you are getting paid for and believe me, it will not go unnoticed. It just doesn't happen that often.**

In an aquarium in Florida there is a tank in which a barracuda and a Spanish mackerel are swimming together peacefully. What makes this unusual is that the Spanish mackerel is the meal of choice for the barracuda. What was done to produce this phenomenon is that a glass barrier was put in the tank with the barracuda on one side and the mackerel on the other. Each time the barracuda would attack the mackerel he would run into the 'invisible' barrier. After many attempts on behalf of the barracuda, he finally gave up trying to attack the mackerel. The glass barrier was then lifted and the barracuda did not attack because he thought the mackerel was still protected. Remember what we learned about 'Behavior Modification'.

You must be careful not to let self-imposed 'invisible' barriers keep you from getting what you WANT.

Become aware of these thought processes and recognize they could be 'Barriers' to important advancements and accomplishments.

> ## Common 'Invisible Barriers'
> - ### Rigid commitment to the past
> - ### Assumption of complete knowledge
> - ### Ignore differences in circumstances
> - ### Over-generalized reactions
> - ### Allow issues to affect Attitude

➤ Rigid commitment to the past –The 'That's how we've always done it' syndrome can keep you from moving forward or worse cause you to fall behind the competition.

➤ Refusal to consider alternatives – Not looking for innovations or seeking recommendations from co-workers, employees or friends may cause you to overlook opportunities.

➤ Over-generalized reactions – Phrases that begin with everyone or no one, e.g. 'Everyone says our prices are too high', this and similar exaggerations are just excuses. Beware.

➤ Assumption of complete knowledge – I've been doing it this way for years. There is no reason to try something new. 'If it ain't broke, don't fix it'. Don't wait until it's too late to fix. Remember the … 'When you are green you grow, when you're ripe you rot' principle.

➤ Ignore differences in circumstances – Changes in the economy or marketplace require a re-assessment of strategies. Ignoring changes can be dangerous.

➤ Inability to function under stress – Avoiding stress and staying within your 'comfort zone' can be a strong deterrent to growth and progress.

## You Yourself, Inc.

**YOU** are the Chairman of the Board

**YOU** own all the stock

**YOU** have Total Management in your hands

**YOU** create your Capitol of Good Will

**YOU** draw on the Interest of Appreciation

**YOU** determine its Worth

**YOU** decide its Success or Failure

A very important analogy to take into consideration is to see ourselves as an individual, independent and productive corporation. You have the complete control and responsibility to make it successful. The net worth of your corporation is determined by the development and improvement of your 'Marketable Assets'.

**Your Inventory of 'Marketable Assets'**

# Knowledge * Experience
# Time Management
# Energy * Initiative * Creativity
# Decision Making
# Goal Setting & Achievement

Your ability to increase your corporation's 'Net Worth', by developing your 'Marketable Assets', is called your potential. It is a fact that your income does not far exceed the personal development of your potential. What are you doing to increase your 'Net Worth'?

What are YOU worth?

How high would you presently rate the market value of your corporation? This individual thinks of himself as having a very high value. He sees his value as a balance wheel for a watch while his friend only sees a bar of iron. Let me explain.

A bar of iron is worth, let's say, $10.

But you mold it into horseshoes the value increases to $30.

You make needles out of it and the value increases to $5,000.

But you make balance wheels for watches out of it and the value increases to $250,000.

The value of raw material is not an indication of what could be its full market value. It's worth is determined by what it becomes.

Who or what do you see yourself becoming that will increase your worth?

Let me share with you how an increase my 'Market Value' paid a big dividend for me. A company I was working with as the Corporate Training Director was bought out by an investment group and they wanted to bring on their own management team. My boss told me of an opportunity that was in my field of expertise, but I would have to become fluent in Spanish. A printing company he knew of had been contracted to print Yellow Pages in Uruguay South America. The problem was that the contract required that they also sell the advertising. They had been looking for a Spanish speaking Yellow Pages sales trainer but they had not found one. I went to New York City for an interview and we agreed on a 90 day consulting contract. I wanted to see if I would like living in South America and it would give them a chance to test my work. I set a goal to increase my 'Market Value' and become fluent in Spanish. The company was pleased with my work and I lived and worked there for 2 years. Upon my return to the U.S., I was able to focus on developing Spanish Yellow Pages in Chicago, Denver, Colorado Springs, Las Vegas, Houston and Phoenix.

What are you doing now to increase your market value?

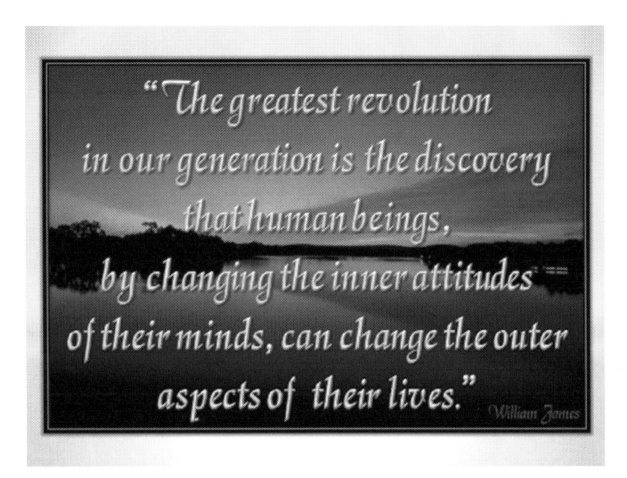

"The greatest revolution in our generation is the discovery that human beings, by changing the inner attitudes of their minds, can change the outer aspects of their lives."
— William James

William James, considered by many as the father of psychology because he was the first educator to offer a psychology course in the United States, understood the important role that attitude plays in determining a person's lifestyle. He firmly believed that a person who understands and takes control of his attitude can actually change their lives.

With what we have covered so far, I sincerely hope that you understand the important role your attitude plays in your life.

Allow me to continue to build my case.

**How important is Attitude?**

**85%** of all **Achievement** is due to **Attitude**
*

**1200 Executives** surveyed to determine the "Key to Success" - **94%** said **Attitude**
*

"It's your **Attitude** not your aptitude that determines your altitude." *Zig Zigler*

Most people never give it a second thought, but without the right attitude many of the advancements and conveniences we now enjoy and take for granted would have never been developed. For progress and growth to take place, it requires people who have the attitude of consistently trying to make things better, more efficient, more rewarding, more pleasurable; just to find ways to improve the status quo. Let me give you a personal example of an improvement I helped make happen, that to me was very rewarding.

After completing the two year project of developing my first Spanish Yellow Pages directory, from concept through implementation, for a company in Chicago, I returned to Phoenix. In 1998 I accepted a position with Wells Fargo Bank as a 'Personal Banker'. Taking advantage of my bi-lingual skills, I was sent to work at a kiosk inside a local grocery store that catered to the Hispanic community. Our main function was to open checking and savings accounts. Two forms of identification were required and many potential customers wanted to use the ID from the Mexican Consulate as a form of identification, but it was not on the list of acceptable ID's. After convincing myself that the 'matricula' met the requirements of proper identification, I approached my supervisor and asked "Why can't we use the ID from the Mexican Consulate as a form of identification?" I was told, "It's not on the list." Being the persistent fellow that I am, I then asked "Why not?" I was told, "I don't know, there must be a reason."

Since no one could tell what the reason was, they finally sent me to the legal liaison, which in turn put me in touch with the corporate legal department in San Francisco. And guess what, the only reason they could give me was that: "No one had ever asked before."

They then asked me to talk with the local consulate, which by the way was excited to participate, to get the criteria required to get the 'matricula'. After reviewing the information, they decided it did meet the identification criteria and decided to use the Phoenix market to test for a possible increased incidence of fraud.

With no evident increase, they decided to expand to other markets. I was then asked to talk to the Mexican Consulate in El Paso, to get their approval to participate in Texas. And so the process began.

An interesting follow-up to this story took place about a year later. I was back in Chicago, having been asked to return to expand on my original project, and while reading the newspaper I saw a headline that featured, 'Bank of America and Bank One now to accept the Mexican Consulate ID to open checking and savings accounts'. I read the article with great interest but, alas, there was no reference of my contribution to the process. But, you can imagine how much pride I felt in knowing I was responsible for helping to initiate the concept.

It is important to note that if I had been working for another organization; one that did not take ideas from their employee's seriously; this process may have taken much longer to implement or maybe not even have originated there. Kudos to the Wells Fargo organization.

1200 executives were surveyed to determine what they felt was the 'Key to Success' and 94% responded with *ATTITUDE* as the key determining factor.

What they knew is that an individual with a *good/positive attitude* has the ability to line up their resources in a constructive and productive manner and direct them towards the achievement of an important objective.

An individual with a *poor/negative attitude* may have the same talents and abilities will lack achievement because they have their resources scattered.

As I often heard Zig Ziglar say; "It's your attitude not your aptitude that determines your altitude." I met Zig Ziglar at one of the very first sales seminars I attended. Needless to say, he was an inspiration. I hope one day, my friend, to "See You at the Top".

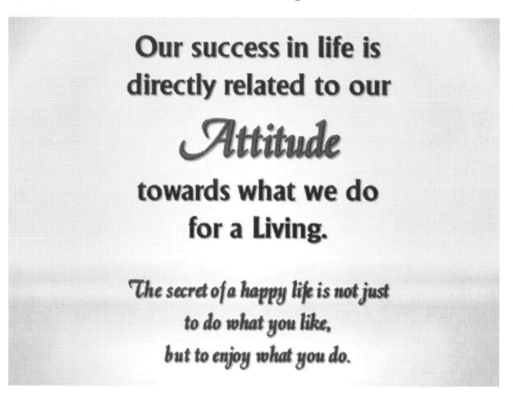

The ideal job or profession would be one in which you truly believe in and which involves something you truly love to do. You should look for ways to keep your work interesting. Almost every job has advancement opportunities that can make the job more interesting. We have already discussed what it takes to get you ready for an advancement opportunity. Always keep trying to find a way to regain the enthusiasm you felt when you first got the position.

If due to bad economic conditions or high unemployment rate you cannot seek a new position readily, then I suggest that you find a hobby or start a new project or you can always volunteer for a community service organization that you believe in. This will bring accomplishment and satisfaction into your life while you look for the right opportunity.

When you volunteer for a community service organization you truly believe in, you will find yourself meeting and making friends with individuals that have similar interests and beliefs. Some of these new contacts may lead you to a referral for just the kind of position you want.

Think positive! The best is yet to come.

This is a list of 100 personality traits and strengths employers said they would like to see in their employees. It is important to recognize that we all have special strengths and due to the fact that each one of us is an 'Original', we exhibit or possess each one of these traits to a certain degree. All of these traits are very admirable and depending on the position that is to be filled some may be more important than others. Of these 100 traits, that we all possess, what percentage do you think are learned skills and what percentage are attitudes?

You may be surprised to know that 90% of the traits are a direct reflection of our attitude.

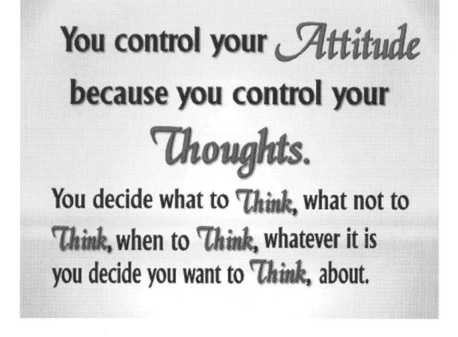

Since 90% of the personality traits most employers are looking for are within our control, we have the power to become the type of person that will be in high demand. We already know that 'We Become What We Think About'…

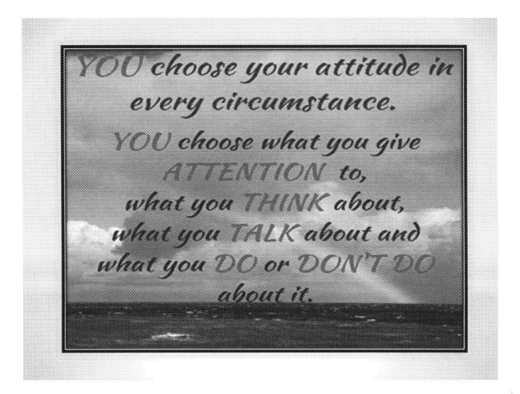

Remember, you don't achieve status or realize accomplishments because of who you would want to be, but because of who you become. Your Life Plan will help you determine who you will become.

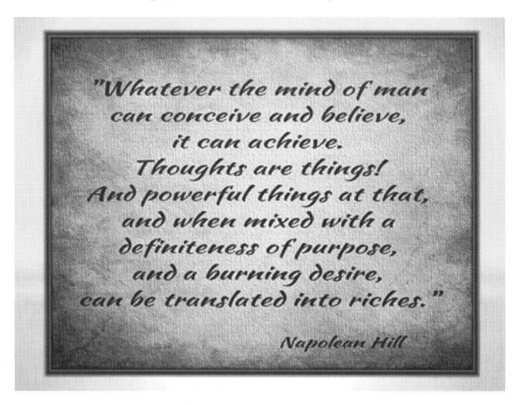

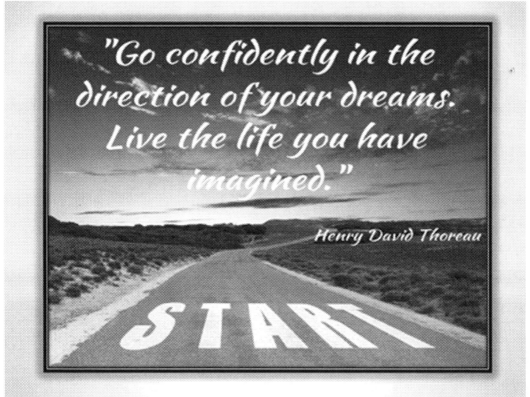

## Without a program for continued
### 'Self Improvement'

➢ **Opportunities –**
**You will lack knowledge and experience**
➢ **Confrontations or Disputes –**
**You won't be a match intellectually**
➢ **Values or Beliefs–**
**Your philosophies & understanding too limited**
**Missing Skills – Missing Knowledge – Missing Insights**
**Will reduce your lifestyle!**

Throughout this discourse I have tried to emphasize the importance of developing a Life Plan and to help you discover that you have the power and the process to take control of your life. It is so important that you give it serious consideration because without a program for continued self-improvement you are going to find that for some opportunities, that might have an important impact on your career, your knowledge and your experience may be lacking. For some confrontations or insightful disputes that you may encounter you won't be a match mentally or intellectually. For some important values or beliefs your philosophies and understanding may be limited.

Missing skills, missing knowledge and missing insights will reduce your lifestyle. Think about it.

George Bernard Shaw was a very well respected author, critic and playwright. He won the Nobel Prize for Literature (1925) and an Oscar (1938) when his play 'Pygmalion' was made into a movie. Years later 'Pygmalion' was turned into the Lerner & Loewe musical 'My Fair Lady', which won much acclaim. Needless to say, Mr. Shaw was on the society A-list.

When he was in his 90's, Mr. Shaw granted an interview in which a reporter asked him a very interesting question; "Mr. Shaw, you have met some very interesting people in your life; royalty, dignitaries, celebrities and politicians. Of all the people you have ever met, if you had your life to live over again, whom would you choose to be?"

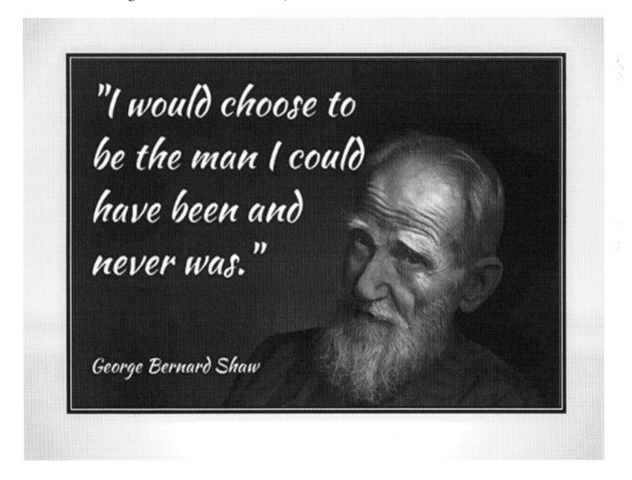

It may be surprising to know that even a man as accomplished as Mr. Shaw recognized he could have done more; he could have been *Better*.

If you had your life to live over, could you do *Better*? Would you make any changes?

Unlike Mr. Shaw who was in his 90's when he made this statement, you and I still have a choice in determining our future.

"Though no one can go back and make a brand new start, anyone can start from now and make a brand new end."

*Carl Bard*

It's not too late to make a change in your life and in your future.

As Zig Ziglar used to say…

"You don't have to be great to start, but you have to start to be GREAT!"

Mr. Ziglar was absolutely right, you do have to START!

I think now is as good a time as any to get started.

What do you think?

Ideas to Think about
- Reach the 'Turning Point' in your life
- Realize you do have untapped 'Potential'
- Accept 'Total Responsibility' for your life
- Choose to be 'Unequal' and develop a Life Plan
- Capitalize on all your 'Special Strengths'
- Expect 'Criticism'
You determine your future because you control your
*Attitude & Thoughts*

May these final thoughts help you in making that most important discovery for yourself; that you reach the *TURNING POINT* in your life and come to the realization that you truly have *UNDEVELOPED POTENTIAL*.; that you will make the decision to take *TOTAL RESPONSIBILITY* for its development; that you choose to become *UNEQUAL* and take the time to develop that essential *LIFE PLAN* to help you get what you *WANT* out of life; that you recognize and capitalize on your *SPECIAL STRENGTHS* and realize that you have the power and the ability to strengthen your weaknesses because you control your thoughts and your thoughts control who you will become.

You can expect *CRITICISM* from people who are afraid to fail in an attempt to improve their lives. They are so afraid to fail, they won't even try, but they will try to dissuade you from doing so. They don't want you to leave them behind; they do not want you to succeed and force them to re-evaluate their lives and their way of thinking. They truly do not have your best interest at heart.

I am going to share with you with one of the most inspiring quotes that I keep in mind on the subject of critics. It is from the 'Rough Rider' himself.

## The Man in the Arena

"It is not the critic who counts, not the man who points out how the strong man stumbles, or where the doer of deeds could have done them better. The credit belongs to the man in the arena, whose face is marred by dust and sweat and blood, who strives valiantly, who knows the great enthusiasms, the great devotions, who spends himself in a worthy cause, who at the best, knows in the end the triumph of high achievement, and, who at the worst, if he fails, at least fails while daring greatly, so that his place shall never be with those cold and timid souls who have never known neither victory or defeat."

Teddy Roosevelt

I sincerely hope that you have made the discovery that a well-structured Life Plan will bring powerful motives into your life and that these motives will give you a reason to take action. Action taken on personal motives is personal motivation.

This is the power of Motives –Your Key to a Successful Future.

# *Motives Action Plan*

## *Workbook Agenda*

# *Inter~Personal Communications Skills*

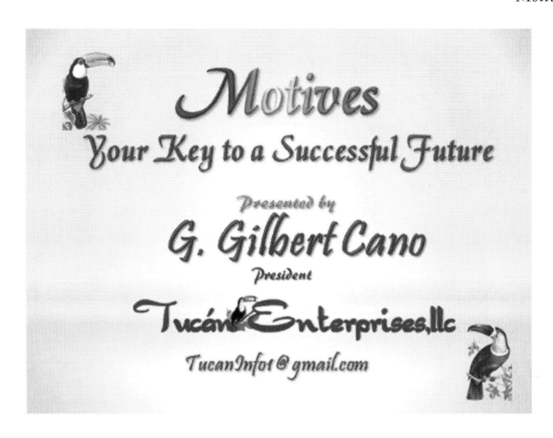

# *Motives Action Plan*

## *Workbook Agenda*

# Action Plan

## For

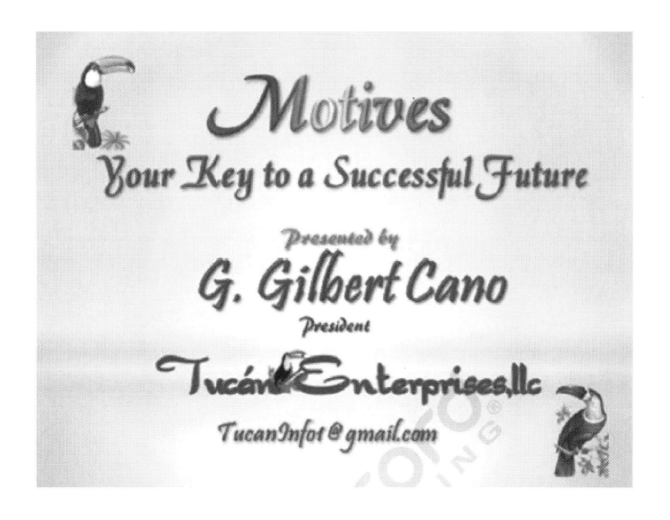

# Motives
## Your Key to a Successful Future

### Table of Contents

*Motives*
*Your Key to a Successful Future*

# Action Plan

## Introduction

I want to congratulate you on reaching that most important **'Turning Point'** in your life. That moment when you realize you really do have undeveloped potential and you make the decision to put a 'Life Plan' into effect to achieve what will be YOUR **personal** idea of success. Only YOU can determine what YOU want to achieve in life. Bear in mind the difference between Wishes and Wants. When we Wish for something, we wait to see if it happens. When we Want something, you will actively find a way to make it happen. Only YOU can decide which **'wants'** will serve as personal 'Motives' to keep you on track and help you <u>persist</u> in the achievement of your full potential.

## Purpose of Action Plan Workbook

This workbook is designed to give you the opportunity to put the concepts you discovered in Motives – Your Key to a Successful Future. This Action Plan is divided into **4 Parts** and will provide you with a step by step system that will allow you to take your time and truly focus on the things YOU really want in life. In this presentation you learned that knowledge is power **<u>only</u>** if it is applied. It is now time to apply the concepts that you have discovered.

**Part 1** of the Action Plan is to create a **'Master Dream List'**. This should be a fun exercise. Set your imagination free. Think as if everything and anything is possible. This program will help you develop a 'Life Plan' that will give you the motivation to turn your 'Master Dream List' into reality.

**Part 2** of the Action Plan is an important **'Self-Appraisal'** that will help you to focus on where you are now in relation to where you want to be. This appraisal will allow you to reflect on some of the most important areas of your life such as: Career, Education, Finances, Health, Spiritual Values, Social Skills and Family Relationships. The insight you will receive with this 'Self-Appraisal' will bring to light areas you may have not previously considered improving. It will become a very important way to track the progress of your personal development.

**Part 3** of the Action Plan is to **'Prioritize'** your **most important goals** in each area. The 'Master Dream List' and the 'Self-Appraisal' will highlight the areas of your life that YOU might want to develop. Only YOU can determine which areas are important to YOU and only YOU can decide which ones will serve as 'Motives' towards helping you to develop more of your full potential.

**Part 4** of the Action Plan is where everything comes together. There are several 'Action Steps' that we must take into consideration with each individual Goal. Completing these action steps will help clarify the purpose and reason you decided to make this Goal important to YOU. People are motivated to do something for one of two reasons; 'Gain a Benefit' or 'Avoid a Loss of something important'. Knowing both is a powerful 'Motive'. Understanding the benefit you will receive from achieving the goal will give you the motivation needed to accomplish it. Understanding the consequences of not achieving the goal will help you stay focused on its achievement. I will explain each step in detail to help you understand their importance in helping you achieve your goals.

I sincerely hope that this 'Action Plan' will help in motivating YOU to develop more of your 'Special Gift' and the unlimited potential you possess. If you will follow these guidelines and **personalize** them to help you develop YOUR 'Life Plan', I know you will enjoy a happier and more eventful life.

One question I am often asked is, "Can you help me manage my time so I can fit this Action Plan into my already full agenda?" I believe that no one can manage time. Time cannot be stopped, controlled or altered in anyway. YOU must learn to manage yourself and that is done by determining and **managing your priorities**. YOU decide what is important in your life. If something is really important to YOU, you will find the time to make it happen. You always have and you always will. It is part of your 'Special Gift'. It is called **Freedom of Choice** and it is up to YOU to decide how you want to utilize the time you are given.

May you continue to develop your 'Master Dream List' and may **YOU** turn all your dreams into reality.

*Gil*

# Part 1—Master Dream List

I like to say, "Most people spend more time planning a vacation than they do planning their lives." They want to make sure they don't miss anything. They think of everything they want to do and see, how much time they will spend in each location and even go on the internet to study the surrounding areas to make sure they don't miss anything. They want to make sure they take full advantage of the time spent on the vacation.

Don't you feel your own life is worth the same time and effort you spend planning a vacation? I am sure you do or you wouldn't be going through this exercise. You're probably thinking, 'Why haven't I done this before now?'

Take your time and write down anything and everything you have ever wanted to do, to have, to become, places you've wanted to visit, etc. Anything and everything should be put on this 'List'. Have fun. Think as if you can have anything your heart desires. Do not let <u>previous conditioning</u> or 'Invisible Barriers' limit you. You will prioritize the list and be more specific, later. It is believed that the 'Human Mind' will not give you a strong desire for something you cannot achieve.

You should come back, review and continue to add to this 'Dream' list throughout the rest of your life. New ideas, opportunities and possibilities will come to light as you grow and develop your potential.

# Part 1—Master Dream List

| Date | | I Want . . . | | Rank |
|------|---|--------------|---|------|
| ———— | \| | ————————————— | \| | ———— |
| ———— | \| | ————————————— | \| | ———— |
| ———— | \| | ————————————— | \| | ———— |
| ———— | \| | ————————————— | \| | ———— |
| ———— | \| | ————————————— | \| | ———— |
| ———— | \| | ————————————— | \| | ———— |
| ———— | \| | ————————————— | \| | ———— |
| ———— | \| | ————————————— | \| | ———— |
| ———— | \| | ————————————— | \| | ———— |
| ———— | \| | ————————————— | \| | ———— |
| ———— | \| | ————————————— | \| | ———— |
| ———— | \| | ————————————— | \| | ———— |
| ———— | \| | ————————————— | \| | ———— |
| ———— | \| | ————————————— | \| | ———— |
| ———— | \| | ————————————— | \| | ———— |
| ———— | \| | ————————————— | \| | ———— |
| ———— | \| | ————————————— | \| | ———— |
| ———— | \| | ————————————— | \| | ———— |
| ———— | \| | ————————————— | \| | ———— |
| ———— | \| | ————————————— | \| | ———— |

# Master Dream List cont.

| Date | | I Want . . . | | Rank |
|------|---|-------------|---|------|
| ———— | \| | ———————————— | \| | ———— |
| ———— | \| | ———————————— | \| | ———— |
| ———— | \| | ———————————— | \| | ———— |
| ———— | \| | ———————————— | \| | ———— |
| ———— | \| | ———————————— | \| | ———— |
| ———— | \| | ———————————— | \| | ———— |
| ———— | \| | ———————————— | \| | ———— |
| ———— | \| | ———————————— | \| | ———— |
| ———— | \| | ———————————— | \| | ———— |
| ———— | \| | ———————————— | \| | ———— |
| ———— | \| | ———————————— | \| | ———— |
| ———— | \| | ———————————— | \| | ———— |
| ———— | \| | ———————————— | \| | ———— |
| ———— | \| | ———————————— | \| | ———— |
| ———— | \| | ———————————— | \| | ———— |
| ———— | \| | ———————————— | \| | ———— |
| ———— | \| | ———————————— | \| | ———— |
| ———— | \| | ———————————— | \| | ———— |
| ———— | \| | ———————————— | \| | ———— |
| ———— | \| | ———————————— | \| | ———— |

# Part 2—Self-Appraisal

As stated previously, this appraisal will allow you to reflect on some of the most important areas of YOUR life such as: Career, Education, Finances, Health, Spiritual Values, Social Skills and Family Relationships. The insight you will receive with this 'Self-Appraisal' will bring to light areas you may have not previously considered improving. You may want to combine two or three statements into one Goal or maybe have two or three Goals in one area. After analyzing the appraisal, YOU will now be able to decide which areas are important to YOU and which areas YOU feel will make you the 'Better' person YOU want to become. YOU will decide their priority in the list of goals you want to achieve.

It is important to seek **balance** in all these areas to help avoid unnecessary stress in your life. It is sad to hear of financially successful people, who lose everything because of poor health, divorce or even worse commit suicide because their total focus was on becoming financially successful at the expense of everything else.

Truthfully rate yourself in regards to each statement with (1) being 'Not like you' to (7) being 'Exactly like you'. Take your time and consider each statement carefully. You do not have to do them all at one sitting. YOUR honest appraisal of your present stage of development is important in helping you determine which areas YOU might want to improve. Highlight the statements in each area that you feel will help you become the better, well rounded and balanced person you want to be. For these goals to serve as 'Motives' in your life, YOU have to determine which ones are important to YOU.

Responding to the statements honestly, might reveal some new items YOU might want to add to your 'Master Dream List'.

Note: (Use pencil) Come back to this 'Self-Appraisal' in a few days and review your responses. Make sure you were as open and honest with yourself as you could be. It is interesting to return to the appraisal in a few months and respond to it again. You will be able to note the progress and growth you have made while working to achieve your most important goals in each area and this will encourage you to persist.

# Part 2—Self-Appraisal

## Physical

| | | | Not like me | | | | | | Exactly like me |
|---|---|---|---|---|---|---|---|---|---|
| 1. | I am in excellent health | | ① | ② | ③ | ④ | ⑤ | ⑥ | ⑦ |
| 2. | I get plenty of rest at night | | ① | ② | ③ | ④ | ⑤ | ⑥ | ⑦ |
| 3. | I have plenty of energy | | ① | ② | ③ | ④ | ⑤ | ⑥ | ⑦ |
| 4. | I eat a balanced diet | | ① | ② | ③ | ④ | ⑤ | ⑥ | ⑦ |
| 5. | My weight is healthy | | ① | ② | ③ | ④ | ⑤ | ⑥ | ⑦ |
| 6. | I exercise regularly | | ① | ② | ③ | ④ | ⑤ | ⑥ | ⑦ |
| 7. | I get a physical check-up regularly | | ① | ② | ③ | ④ | ⑤ | ⑥ | ⑦ |
| 8. | I do not smoke cigarettes | | ① | ② | ③ | ④ | ⑤ | ⑥ | ⑦ |
| 9. | I do not drink alcohol excessively | | ① | ② | ③ | ④ | ⑤ | ⑥ | ⑦ |
| 10. | Stress and tension at work do not affect my physical well being | | ① | ② | ③ | ④ | ⑤ | ⑥ | ⑦ |
| 11. | I handle all my obligations without excessive worry or stress | | ① | ② | ③ | ④ | ⑤ | ⑥ | ⑦ |
| 12. | I maintain a healthy balance between work, recreation, social and family life | | ① | ② | ③ | ④ | ⑤ | ⑥ | ⑦ |
| 13. | I have specific goals to maintain my physical well-being | | ① | ② | ③ | ④ | ⑤ | ⑥ | ⑦ |

## Intellectual

Not like me ☞　　Exactly like me ☜

1. I am an intelligent individual　① ② ③ ④ ⑤ ⑥ ⑦
2. I consider myself well educated　① ② ③ ④ ⑤ ⑥ ⑦
3. I am creative　① ② ③ ④ ⑤ ⑥ ⑦
4. I enjoy finding ways to improve the status quo　① ② ③ ④ ⑤ ⑥ ⑦
5. I enjoy learning new things　① ② ③ ④ ⑤ ⑥ ⑦
6. I have adequate skills and knowledge to be successful in my work　① ② ③ ④ ⑤ ⑥ ⑦
7. I recognize some areas in which increased knowledge and skills could improve my lifestyle　① ② ③ ④ ⑤ ⑥ ⑦
8. I am interested in other subjects besides my work　① ② ③ ④ ⑤ ⑥ ⑦

## Social

Not like me ☞　　Exactly like me ☜

1. I enjoy social gatherings　① ② ③ ④ ⑤ ⑥ ⑦
2. I have many friends　① ② ③ ④ ⑤ ⑥ ⑦
3. I have a good sense of humor　① ② ③ ④ ⑤ ⑥ ⑦
4. I am comfortable introducing myself to new people　① ② ③ ④ ⑤ ⑥ ⑦
5. I make friends easily　① ② ③ ④ ⑤ ⑥ ⑦
6. I am self-confident　① ② ③ ④ ⑤ ⑥ ⑦
7. I am a leader　① ② ③ ④ ⑤ ⑥ ⑦
8. I can follow as well as lead　① ② ③ ④ ⑤ ⑥ ⑦
9. I care about other people　① ② ③ ④ ⑤ ⑥ ⑦
10. I enjoy helping others　① ② ③ ④ ⑤ ⑥ ⑦
11. I enjoy sharing ideas with others　① ② ③ ④ ⑤ ⑥ ⑦

## Financial

1. I am conscientious with my financial affairs — ① ② ③ ④ ⑤ ⑥ ⑦
2. I have an excellent credit rating — ① ② ③ ④ ⑤ ⑥ ⑦
3. I use a personal/family budget — ① ② ③ ④ ⑤ ⑥ ⑦
4. I regularly save part of my income — ① ② ③ ④ ⑤ ⑥ ⑦
5. My earnings have increased progressively for the past five years — ① ② ③ ④ ⑤ ⑥ ⑦
6. I am satisfied with my current income — ① ② ③ ④ ⑤ ⑥ ⑦
7. I expect to earn more and increase my net worth in the future — ① ② ③ ④ ⑤ ⑥ ⑦
8. I have set specific goals and plans for my financial future — ① ② ③ ④ ⑤ ⑥ ⑦
9. I have specific plans for further advancement in my career — ① ② ③ ④ ⑤ ⑥ ⑦

## Spiritual

1. My spiritual and ethical values are important to me — ① ② ③ ④ ⑤ ⑥ ⑦
2. I sincerely practice my religious beliefs — ① ② ③ ④ ⑤ ⑥ ⑦
3. I am one who can be trusted — ① ② ③ ④ ⑤ ⑥ ⑦
4. I am an honest, law abiding citizen — ① ② ③ ④ ⑤ ⑥ ⑦
5. My character is constantly improving — ① ② ③ ④ ⑤ ⑥ ⑦
6. I have a sense of purpose in life — ① ② ③ ④ ⑤ ⑥ ⑦
7. It is important for me to help others — ① ② ③ ④ ⑤ ⑥ ⑦
8. I would prefer rejection than sacrifice my principles — ① ② ③ ④ ⑤ ⑥ ⑦

## *Family Relationships*

1. I openly demonstrate love, courtesy and respect for each family member   ① ② ③ ④ ⑤ ⑥ ⑦

2. I maintain open communication with each family member   ① ② ③ ④ ⑤ ⑥ ⑦

3. I respect the right of each family member to hold beliefs and opinions that are different from mine   ① ② ③ ④ ⑤ ⑥ ⑦

4. I can agree to disagree with family members without unpleasant scenes   ① ② ③ ④ ⑤ ⑥ ⑦

5. I can forgive and forget after a disagreement or quarrel with a family member   ① ② ③ ④ ⑤ ⑥ ⑦

6. My attitude and behavior helps other family members develop self-esteem and self-respect   ① ② ③ ④ ⑤ ⑥ ⑦

7. I spend quality time with members of my family   ① ② ③ ④ ⑤ ⑥ ⑦

8. I have specific goals for fulfilling my role in the family   ① ② ③ ④ ⑤ ⑥ ⑦

Note: Try giving yourself an honest overall rating in each category, comparing where you are now as to where you really think you should be. You could use 1-10 scale.

Physical ___         Financial ___

Intellectual ___ Spiritual ___

Social ___        Family Relationships ___

Consider each category as a spoke in the wheel of your

'YOU-ni Cycle'. If they are not balanced, it might let you know why your 'ride through life' is a little bumpy.

# Part 3—My #1 Goals

The 'Freedom of Choice' to decide for yourself what is important to YOU is part of your 'Special Gift'. One of the main principles behind the concept of Motive-The Key to Success and the secret to developing long term enthusiasm and self-motivation is for YOU to determine what YOU want out of life. Only YOU can determine which goals will serve as 'Motives' to give you the enthusiasm and power to persist.

It is at this point that we want to move for generalities to specifics. "I want to be successful", will not motivate you if you do not define exactly what being successful means to YOU. What specifically needs to happen for you to know that you are successful? That is what will define your goal. The same applies to all generalities. "I want to be happy" is not attainable until YOU decide exactly what happiness means to YOU. You would be surprised to find how few people really know what they WANT out of life. Not knowing what you really WANT out of life, makes it difficult to stay excited, enthusiastic and self-motivated.

After reviewing your now more personal 'Master Dream List' and with the insights from your 'Self-Appraisal', it is now time to prioritize your Goals. Sometimes you can be overwhelmed by wanting to achieve everything at once. That is why I recommend picking your #1most important Goal in each area to start. I don't want you to get caught up in the 'Paralysis by Analysis' syndrome and stop the process because you can't decide which one is most important. Since they are all goals you want to accomplish, pick one that you feel is special in each of the areas that you have decided you want to improve. You will eventually be working to accomplish all YOUR Goals but it is important to become familiar with the process.

Remember what Zig Ziglar says,

*"You don't have to be great to start, but you have to start to be Great."*

# Part 3—My #1 Goals

*Focus on this list to start. You will add more*
*Goals as these are achieved.*

My #1 *Personal Goal* is: _____

_____

My #1 *Self-Improvement Goal* is: _____

_____

My #1 *Business Goal* is: _____

_____

My #1 *Financial Goal* is: _____

_____

My #1 *Intellectual Goal* is: _____

_____

My #1 *Social Goal* is: _____

_____

My #1 *Family Goal* is: _____

_____

My #1 *Spiritual Goal* is: _____

_____

My #1 *Physical Goal* is: _____

_____

# Part 4—A 'Motive' for My Success

Knowing what you WANT and developing a specific PLAN to attain it will help YOU develop an 'I can do that' attitude. This attitude will help you develop the DESIRE and the commitment to overcome minor setbacks and you will outperform even your own expectations. This performance will give YOU the CONFIDENCE to try new ideas and to BELIEVE IN YOURSELF. Remember, you can always succeed even if no one else believes in you, but never if you don't believe in yourself. Knowing what you WANT in life will give you purpose and 'Motive'. It will change your life.

## Action Plan

**Step 1**—Goal Statement

Write down your **Goal**, bearing in mind the characteristics of the SMART system that was discussed. It has to be **Specific**, it must be **Measurable**, you must be able to assume **Accountability** and accept responsibility for its achievement and it should be **Realistic** and relevant. Later, you will develop a **Timeline** with specific action steps and a target date for the completion of each step.

## Step 2—*Benefit Received from Achievement*

Identify the **Benefits** that you will receive from achieving the Goal. This is a very important part of the process. How YOU will benefit from achieving this Goal will determine how strong a 'Motive' you will have to persist and overcome setbacks. This will help YOU determine how important this Goal is to YOU.

## Step 3—*Consequences of Non-Achievement*

It is also important to think about what can happen if YOU don't achieve this Goal. Remember, the two strongest motives for doing something are to 'Gain a Benefit' or 'Avoid a Loss'. Recognizing some advantage or capacity you might lose in the future can be just as motivating as gaining a benefit. Give this some thought.

## Step 4—*Possible Obstacles*

It is important to try and identify **Possible Obstacles**. One good way to avoid setbacks is to prepare for them ahead of time. Completing this exercise now will give you time to think of a strategy to overcome these obstacles which you will address the next step.

## Step 5—*Possible Solutions for Obstacles*

When you take the time to develop a strategy for overcoming a possible obstacle with a **Possible Solution** to the obstacles you are in essence eliminating that obstacle. That is why it is important to take the time to go through these two steps of the process.

## Step 6—*Affirmations*

**Affirmations** are designed to help maintain positive thoughts in your mind towards the achievement of the goal by using spaced repetition on our sub-conscious. Remember, <u>'We become what we think about'</u>. An affirmation is a positive declaration of a goal we want to achieve, stated as if it already a reality. They should be selected and designed for your private use. Since we use affirmations to try to impress upon the sub-conscious a more ideal and desirable imagery, the wording we use is very important.

A well written affirmation will be stated positively, in the present tense and include the personal pronoun 'I'. Use 'feeling' words that are comfortable to you and when possible specify your wording.

Affirmations should be practical and use realistic standards like 'consistently' or 'regularly' and not inflexible ones like 'always' and 'every time'. Some examples are:

"I like and respect myself."
"I weigh 180 pounds and feel terrific."
"I consistently save 10% of my paycheck."
"I am a caring spouse."
"I keep up with current events."
"I exercise daily"

## Step 7—*Action Steps for Achieving this Goal*

Identify specific **Action Steps** to be taken to achieve the Goal. Break down the main Goal into smaller, measurable steps. For example, what pre-requisites must be completed or what progress do you expect to make in a week, or a month, or in three months increments depending on the Goal. Successfully completing smaller goals helps develop the 'I can do it' attitude. These Action Steps set a **Timeline** for the Goal.

## Step 8—*Set a Target Date for Achieving each Step*

By setting a **Target Date** for each step we are making a commitment to take action. Bear in mind, these target dates are not set in stone. They are only a method of keeping track of your progress. If you did not successfully complete the step by your Target Date, you need to identify the reasons for not accomplishing the step on time. This is a reality check on your commitment to achieving the Goal. Look for obstacles that you may have not taken into consideration when you first set the Target Date. Taking this new information into consideration, you just reset the date and move forward. Do not consider this a failure. Remember 'You only fail when you stop trying'.

## Step 9— *Visualization*

**Visualization** of your goal is a very important way to help you sustain your motivation. A clear picture in your mind of the goal you are trying to reach is one more way to get the sub-conscious to work <u>for</u> you. You can use models, photographs, brochures or anything that will symbolize the goals you have set. Look at them every day and picture yourself already having achieved the Goal. Because of the positive affirmation you receive in visualizing your accomplished goal, you experience an increase in energy and the motivation to persist in making your goal a reality.

<u>Lastly,</u> answer the question, "Is it **worth** my time, money and effort to reach this Goal?" If you cannot sincerely answer in the affirmative, skip it and go on to the next Goal.

Note: Refer to the above description of the process as you complete the following exercises.

# A 'Motive' for My Success

Date                    Target Date                    Date Achieved

Goal Statement

_____

_____

_____

Benefit Received from Achievement

_____

_____

_____

Consequences of Non~Achievement

_____

_____

_____

## Possible Obstacles

_____

_____

_____

## Possible Solutions for Obstacles

_____

_____

_____

## Affirmations

_____

_____

_____

## Action Steps for Achieving this Goal

1.) _____

_____

2.) _____

_____

3.) _____

_____

## Target Date ☑

_____ ☐

_____ ☐

_____ ☐

4.) _____     _____ ☐

_____

5.) _____     _____ ☐

_____

6.) _____     _____ ☐

_____

7.) _____     _____ ☐

_____

8.) _____     _____ ☐

_____

*Is it worth my time, money and effort to reach this goal?*

☐ *Yes* ☐ *No* ☐ *Later*

102

# Inter~Personal Communications Skills

*Inter-personal Communications*

*Discovery Phase*
Who – What – Where – When – Why – How
*Presentation Phase*
Features – Benefits
*Decision Phase (Negotiation)*
✓ Listen to their point of view
✓ Re-phrase to clarify assumptions
✓ Demonstrate understanding
✓ Present your view
✓ Get agreement

All new conversations start with the Discovery Phase in which begin with trying to find out who they are, what do they do, where they are from, when did they become interested in what they do, etc. Then we tell them about ourselves. Then using negotiation tactics, we try to determine if we want to establish a relationship. We need to bear in mind that with both participants in the conversation 55% of the conversation is conveyed by our body language our eyes and facial expressions. 38% by the tone of the voice, it's intensity of delivery and the style that is used. Only 7% is conveyed by the words we use. That is why you need to learn how to ask questions and listen with sincere interest to be able to control the conversation.

In sales there many benefits to asking questions. The following is a list of reasons as to why asking questions in sales is important. Many of them apply to everyday conversations. Be aware of the benefits and use them when appropriate.

## Why Ask Questions?

1.) **Control** – By asking questions you control the conversation

2.) **Involvement** – Creating a dialogue will give you insight on how proceed

3.) **Get Yeses** – Asking agreeable questions helps build comfort zone

4.) **Determine Interest** – Have you ever thought of...?

5.) **Clarify** – Could you tell me a little more about why that is a concern ...?

6.) **Isolate Objections** – Is there any other reason ...?

7.) **Maintain Rapport** – Don't you agree...? or Does that make sense to you?

8.) **Understand Strategy** – What are your plans for growth this year?

9.) **Create Concern** – How can your competition affect your business?

10.) **Get Commitments** – Are you ready to move forward...?

It is also very important that you develop the art of creative listening. Have the proper attitude and a sincere interest in the person you are talking to.

## The Art of Creative Listening

### Proper Awareness

✓ Avoid Preoccupation with Personal Problems
✓ Avoid Arguing Mentally
✓ Use Reflective Feedback to Check for Understanding
✓ Control Temptation to Interrupt & Avoid Jumping to Conclusions
✓ Write Down Important Points, Questions or Comments
✓ Acknowledge Understanding with Smile, Nod or Interjection
✓ Difference in Rate of Speech (100 to 150 words per minute)
vs.
Rate of Thinking (250 to 500 words per minute)

It is very important to have the proper awareness on your part. Don't let personal problems distract you from giving your full attention and avoid trying to think of how you are going to rebuttal an idea you are in disagreement with. This distraction might cause you to miss something very important to the conversation. If something is said you are not quite sure of, always ask; "Let me make sure that I understand what you are saying, do you mean that..." This will only show that you are sincerely interested in what they are saying and want to avoid jumping to conclusions. Try to control the temptation to interrupt and acknowledge understanding with a smile, nod or interjection.

What many people tend to forget is that the difference between the Rate of Speech (100 to 150 words/minute) and Rate of Thinking (250 to 500 words/minute) sometimes causes the mind to wander. I'm sure it's happened to you that during a conversation you think of something you need to do or something you did which was not even related to the conversation. The same can happen to the other person. An important point that you or that the other person has made might get lost in the conversation if you are not constantly aware of this phenomenon.

## The Influence of Personality

The ability to recognize 'Personality' traits will help increase your percentage of positive and productive encounters & also help you understand how to best relate with someone.

This particular subject is so important that many books have written to explain it. I have read books where the personalities are divided into six; eight even ten groups. Some authors will group the personalities by color, tribes and different acronyms. They all understand the importance of the subject and just try to find different ways to explain it so you can take advantage of it. I use what I consider the main four. My goal is just to make you aware of the importance of recognizing the different personalities and hope that I can generate enough interest for you to want to read more of the books that cover the subject in-depth.

*Descriptive Trait Groups*

**To be most effective in Inter-personal Communications we must 1st understand our own *'Personal Traits'*.**

We all have different ways of processing and explaining information. It gets to be a problem when you expect someone to accept your way of thinking about and explaining a topic. As we will learn, this is not true.

If you are what is considered a Driver, you don't believe is wasting time with details. You just want to get to the bottom line. But, if you are talking to someone who has an Amiable personality, they tend to be very cautious and need a lot of information and detail to be convinced. You being a Driver feel that it is a waste of time and don't feel that details are necessary. What do you think are the chances of them being able to communicate effectively?

Another example: suppose you have an Expressive personality. You will have a tendency to want to talk a lot, tell stories, build a friendly relationship and in general feel that dealing with numbers is cold. But, if you are talking to an Analytical, their comfort level is dealing with facts and figures. They want to be able to justify any decision they make with the proof of logic. What are their chances of being able to communicate effectively?

As you can see, being able to understand how the person you are talking to processes information can be important. I have had experienced sales reps that I have trained say: "I wish I had learned this several years ago. I understand now how I lost some sales that I know I should have made." It's never too late to learn something new.

The first step is to learn what your main type of personality is. We all have all four of the personalities to some degree but there is one that is dominant.

To determine your dominant personality type, I have included a quick survey. This is by no means the best survey, there are some that are very sophisticated but this one is simple to use. It is important that you answer the questions honestly. Circle the two of the four choices given on each line which best describe how you are now, not how you would like to be perceived. If you respond honestly and sincerely you will be surprised at how realistic it can be.

# Descriptive Trait Groups
Circle two choices, per line, across the four columns

| <u>W</u> | <u>X</u> | <u>Y</u> | <u>Z</u> |
|---|---|---|---|
| Task-Oriented | Decisive | Relations | Cautious |

# Descriptive Trait Groups

| W | X | Y | Z |
|---|---|---|---|
| Practical | Aggressive | Empathetic | Non-assertive |
| Self-Controlled | Authoritative | Shows Emotions | Thorough |
| Goal-Directed | Assertive | Gregarious | Patient |
| Methodical | Unhesitating | Sincere | Prudent |
| All-Business | Bold | Personable | Deliberate |
| Organized | Telling | Courteous | Listening |
| Industrious | Independent | Companionable | Cooperative |
| No-Nonsense | Decided | Talkative | Reflective |
| Serious | Resolute | Warm | Careful |
| To-the-Point | Risk-Taker | Amiable | Moderate |
| Business-Like | Definite | Sociable | Precise |
| Diligent | Firm | Demonstrative | Particular |
| Systematic | Strong-Minded | Sense of Humor | Thinking |
| Formal | Confident | Expressive | Hesitative |
| Persevering | Forceful | Trusting | Restrained |
|  |  |  |  |

You will notice that the columns in the Descriptive Trait Groups are labeled W, X, Y, Z. Add up the circles in each column and place the number in the boxes below the columns. Transfer those numbers to the Tally Section of the Behavior Style Graph. Next you will put an x on each line labeled W X Y X on the graph at the appropriate number. You will then make a square using the marked spots as a guide. I will show you what my graph looked like, to give you an idea of what the square should look like.

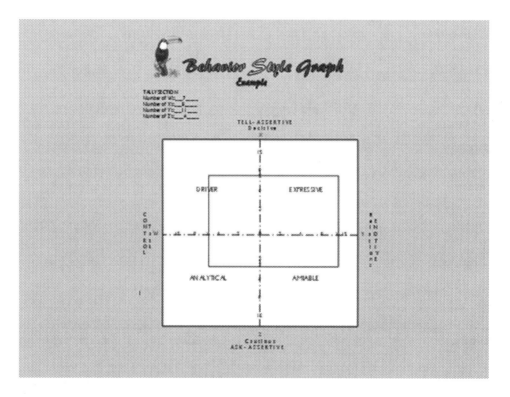

As you can see, my dominant trait is Expressive with Driver second, Amiable being third and Analytical being the least. Which shows; I like to talk a lot and be in control.

As I mentioned we all have all four traits but one is always dominant. Depending on the work you do, some traits are more important than others. Not better, just more important. For example, an accountant should have a higher analytical trait. Let's take a look at some of the highlights of each trait. As I mentioned before this not as sophisticated as some tests but it should give a good idea of how the concept works and maybe you will want to learn more about it.

110

*Behavior Style Graph*

**TALLY SECTION**

Number of Ws:_____
Number of X's:_____
Number of Y's:_____
Number of Z's:_____

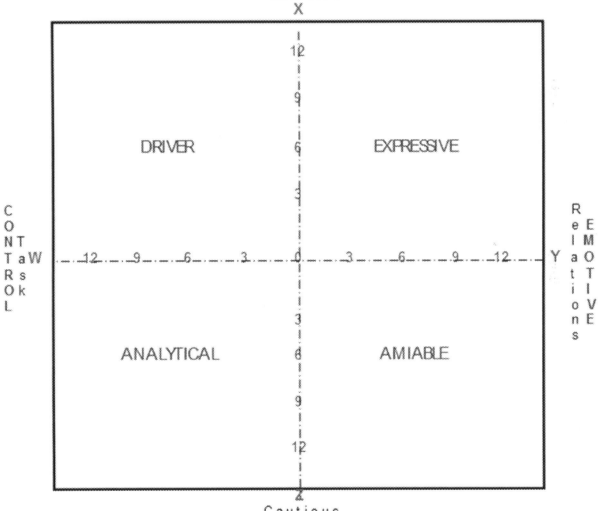

TELL-ASSERTIVE
Decisive
X

DRIVER          EXPRESSIVE

CONTROL          Relations EMOTIVE

ANALYTICAL          AMIABLE

Cautious
ASK-ASSERTIVE

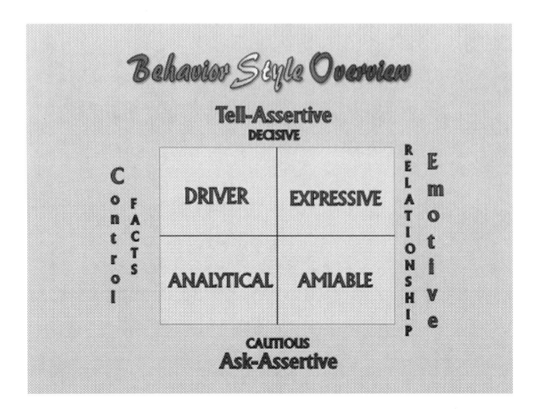

Let me give you a quick overview of what the graph shows us.

The Driver and Expressive personalities are Tell-Assertive. This means they will try to dominate the conversation and tell you what needs to be done. They are also good at making a decision without having to consult with anyone.

The Expressive and Amiable side shows they depend on their instincts and emotions. They feel comfortable talking to someone and try to build a relationship before making a decision.

The Analytical and Amiable side shows they are cautious and Ask-Assertive. This means they ask questions until they are satisfied that they have enough information to make a decision.

The Driver and Analytical side shows they like to maintain control of the conversation and are more interested in facts and figures. They like to think their decisions are based on logic. Not interested as much in relationship building.

Let's take a closer look at the characteristics and communication strategies for each type of personality. I am going to use the slides from my sales training presentation and I will expand just a little on each.

## Characteristics of
## DRIVER

Controlling – Competitive – Achiever

Inquisitive – Impatient – Self-starter

Assertive – Direct – Impulsive
Voice-mail: Curt and brief

## Communication Strategies
## DRIVER

✓Be clear, specific, brief and to the point; use time to be efficient
✓Stick to business; give high points
✓Be prepared with all support materials in a well organized 'package'
✓Present the facts logically; plan your presentation efficiently
✓Ask specific questions; try to solve a problem
✓Provide alternatives and choices for making decisions
✓Provide facts and figures about the probability of success or
   effectiveness of options
✓If you disagree, take issue with facts, not the person
✓Motivate and persuade by referring to objectives
✓End result not process
✓"As you already know..." is a good way of presenting new ideas

As you can tell the driver has unique characteristics and is probably one of the easiest to communicate with because they will tell you what they need to know. They don't like to waste time and are interested in getting to the bottom line.

## Characteristics of
# EXPRESSIVE

Charismatic - Influential - Affable

Verbal - Persuasive - Impetuous

Active - Energetic - Impulsive
Voice-mail: Friendly and long

## Communication Strategies
# EXPRESSIVE

✓ Very important to develop the relationship
✓ Offer special, immediate and extra incentives for their willingness to take action
✓ Plan interaction that supports their dreams and intuitions
✓ Use time to be complimentary, stimulating, fast moving
✓ Focus on purpose of visit; leave time for relating and socializing
✓ Talk about and their goals; opinions they find stimulating
✓ Don't talk details; put them in writing; pin them to modes of action
✓ Ask for their opinions and ideas regarding concept
✓ Provide ideas for implementing

An Expressive is a 'people person' verbal and charismatic. They like to talk; it's their way of getting to know you. It is very important to develop a relationship with this type of person. They are turned off by people that try to impress them with just facts and figures. They like to share their opinion. They can be very persuasive.

114

## Characteristics of
## ANALYTICAL

*Disciplined - Careful - Systematic*

*Self-conscious - Accurate - Logical*

*Reserved - Suspicious - Serious*
*Voice-mail: Detailed*

## Communication Strategies
## ANALYTICAL

✓ Prepare your presentation in advance; take the time to be accurate
✓ Approach them in a straightforward, conservative, direct way; stick to business
✓ Stress loss or risk if action not taken; no hard sell or wild claims
✓ Build your credibility listing pros and cons to any suggestion made
✓ Make an organized contribution to their goals
✓ Draw up a scheduled approach to implementing action with a step by step timetable
✓ Assure them there won't be any surprises; cautious and suspicious of unsupported claims
✓ Provide solid, tangible practical evidence; yes or no answers not good enough
✓ Present specifics and do what you say you will do

An Analytical is very systematic and accurate. They are suspicious by nature and are more impressed by facts and figures. They like to be able to prove that their decisions are based on facts and are very logical. Anyone should be able to agree with any decision they make because they have the facts to prove they are right.

## Characteristics of AMIABLE

Dependable ~ Deliberate ~ Understanding

Conservative ~ Good listener ~ Hesitant

Overly cautious ~ Peaceful ~ Easy-going
Voice-mail: Soft and helpful

## Communication Strategies AMIABLE

✓ Establish friendship and trust; show interest in them as people; be candid and open
✓ Present your case softly, non-threateningly; move ahead casually and informally
✓ Start (briefly) with a personal commitment; establish trustworthiness
✓ Ask questions to draw their opinions; listen and be responsive
✓ Define process clearly with individual contribution; stress service
✓ Provide personal assurances, clear specific solutions with maximum guarantees
✓ Assure them their decision will have minimum risks and provide maximum benefits

An Amiable is a good listener but is overly cautious. Their biggest concern is being taken advantage of. It is important to give them personal assurance and speak in a slow and non-threatening manner. They are generally slow in making decisions because they fear they might make a wrong one. They are by nature conservative and dependable. Developing a good relationship is very important to them.

116

Although this was just a brief insight into the importance of understanding Inter-Personal communications, I hope that it has sparked enough interest for you to want to learn more about the subject. Once you know what to look for, asking questions and listening to how they respond will become second nature to you and almost like a game. You will become a much better conversationalist.

I sincerely hope you have found this book enlightening and will continue to grow into becoming the best you can be. Enjoy a wonder filled and successful future.

The best way to practice your new communications skills is by attending 'Networking Mixers'. Try to engage people you don't know. See if you can determine their 'Personality Type' by their responses to your questions. Knowing your 'Personality Type', make sure you adjust your questions to make them feel comfortable and establish 'Rapport', see how long you can keep them talking. Remember:

*'He who talks dominates the conversation.*
*He who listens controls the conversation.'*

Let me share some ideas as to why developing your networking skills is important.

**Benefits of attending the Networking 'Mixers'**

✓ Meet prospective business clients
✓ Meet other professionals with similar interests
✓ Meet future business partnerships
✓ Meet prospects for future, long term business referral relationships

## How to Effectively 'Work a Mixer'

1.) Adjust Attitude & Look for 'Centers of Influence'
2.) 'Personal Introduction' & Ask for Business Card
3.) Engage in Conversation
4.) Ask 'Feel Good' Questions
5.) Ask the one 'Key' Question
6.) Revisit new contacts later using their name
7.) Introduce them to other attendees
8.) Follow-up with a 'Note'

It is important to note that each 'Center of Influence' has at least 200 people in their circle. Centers of Influence are easily spotted. They are the ones leading discussions and surrounded by other networkers.

Personal Introductions should employ the KISS principle, Keep It Short and Simple. Not a sales pitch of any kind.

Always ask for Business Card. You will use it later when you follow-up with a Note saying you enjoyed meeting them. If they seem like a potential client ask for a follow-up meeting.

Engage in conversation by asking easy questions like:

> *How did you get started in the business?*
> *What do you like most about your business?*

Always ask: *How would I know if someone I'm talking to might be a good prospect for you?*

Try to re-visit later using their name and if possible introduce them to other attendees.

Always remember the Law of Reciprocity – *If you truly help others, someone will eventually help you.*

Once you hone you communication skills you will enjoy the opportunity to meet new people. Plus you will add to your list of clients that can give you referrals.

## The Importance of Referrals from established clients:

### Referrals are 'Preferred' Prospects

- ✓ **Referred prospects are a better quality prospect because of shared influence and shared trust.**
- ✓ **Positioned as referral-based salesperson**
- ✓ **Gives the prospect advantage of indirect experience**
- ✓ **Builds loyalty of person who referred you**

As you can see there are many benefits of 'Referrals'. There are also risks inherent to your client who gives you referrals.

## Risk Inherent in Referrals

**1st - For a client to give you a referral, they must be willing to risk their relationship with the referred person or business.**

**2nd - If you are not Referable (Risk Free) you place your client in an awkward and uncomfortable position.**

You must protect your client.

## Elements That Make You 'Referable'

✓ **Friendly Relationship**
✓ **Established Trust** (You will protect referral's interest.)
✓ **Proven Reliability** (In you and your product.)
✓ **Considered Knowledgeable in your field**
✓ **Considered a Resource to your client**

## Business Referral Axiom

*All things being equal, people will do business with and refer business to someone they Know, Like and Trust.*

It has been my pleasure to share the insights featured throughout this book because, as you can see by my examples, they worked for me. I sincerely hope that some of the concepts will help you reach that 'Turning Point' and give the push you need to sincerely strive to be the 'Better You.' See how much you can really achieve if you gave it your best.

I always remember what Galileo said:

*'You cannot teach a man the truth.*
*You can only help him discover it for himself.'*

I sincerely hope you have made the *'Discovery'* for yourself. I wish you continued Success and a wonder-filled and exciting future.

*Gil Cano*

# Motives
## Your Key to a Successful Future

Presented by

# G. Gilbert Cano

President

# Tucán Enterprises, llc

TucanInfo1@gmail.com

Printed in the United States
By Bookmasters